Pan-India Stories of Informal Workers During Covid-19 Pandemic

Deepanshu Mohan · Sakshi Chindaliya ·
Arun Kumar Kaushik
Editors

Pan-India Stories of Informal Workers During Covid-19 Pandemic

Crisis Narratives

palgrave
macmillan

Editors
Deepanshu Mohan
Centre for New Economics Studies,
Jindal School of Liberal Arts
and Humanities
O.P. Jindal Global University
Sonipat, Haryana, India

Sakshi Chindaliya
Jindal School of Liberal Arts
and Humanities
O.P. Jindal Global University
Sonipat, Haryana, India

Arun Kumar Kaushik
Jindal School of Liberal Arts
and Humanities
O.P. Jindal Global University
Sonipat, Haryana, India

ISBN 978-981-97-1524-4 ISBN 978-981-97-1525-1 (eBook)
https://doi.org/10.1007/978-981-97-1525-1

This Palgrave Macmillan imprint is published by the registered company Springer Nature Singapore Pte Ltd.
The registered company address is: 152 Beach Road, #21-01/04 Gateway East, Singapore 189721, Singapore

Paper in this product is recyclable.

Contents

List of Contributors

Sakshi Chindaliya Jindal School of Liberal Arts and Humanities, O.P. Jindal Global University, Sonipat, India

Shubhangi Derhgawen Centre for New Economics Studies, Jindal School of Liberal Arts and Humanities, O.P. Jindal Global University, Sonipat, India;
Centre for Modern Indian Studies, Georg-August-Universität, Göttingen, Germany

Arun Kumar Kaushik Jindal School of Liberal Arts and Humanities, O.P. Jindal Global University, Sonipat, India

Jignesh Mistry Centre for New Economics Studies, Jindal School of Liberal Arts And Humanities, Jindal Global University, Sonipat, India

Hima Trisha Mohan Centre for New Economics Studies, Jindal School of Liberal Arts and Humanities, O.P. Jindal Global University, Sonipat, India;
Jindal Global Law School, Sonipat, India

Deepanshu Mohan Centre for New Economics Studies, Jindal School of Liberal Arts and Humanities, O.P. Jindal Global University, Sonipat, India

Rishiraj Sen Indian Institute of Management Ahmedabad, Ahmedabad, India

Ashika Thomas London School of Economics and Political Science, London, UK

List of Figures

Chapter 3

CHAPTER 1

Introduction

Sakshi Chindaliya, Ashika Thomas, Deepanshu Mohan, and Arun Kumar Kaushik

Abstract In the aftermath of the COVID-19 pandemic, the global landscape underwent a profound transformation, revealing the fragility of existing systems and prompting a critical reevaluation of alliances, power structures, and information dissemination. This introductory

S. Chindaliya (✉) · D. Mohan · A. K. Kaushik
Jindal School of Liberal Arts and Humanities, O.P. Jindal Global University, Sonipat, India
e-mail: sakshichindaliya@yahoo.in

D. Mohan
e-mail: dmohan@jgu.edu.in

A. K. Kaushik
e-mail: akkaushik@jgu.edu.in

D. Mohan
Centre for New Economics Studies, Jindal School of Liberal Arts And Humanities, Jindal Global University, Sonipat, O.P, India

A. Thomas
London School of Economics and Political Science, London, UK
e-mail: ashikathms@gmail.com

D. Mohan et al. (eds.), *Pan-India Stories of Informal Workers During Covid-19 Pandemic*, https://doi.org/10.1007/978-981-97-1525-1_1

chapter explores the implications of the pandemic on India, particularly its marginalised communities inhabiting informal spaces, as the crisis accentuated existing disparities. Spanning diverse geographies and demographics, the chapter introduces contexts and concepts used to unpack the intricate socio-economic, gender, and caste dimensions that shape the lives of marginalised groups in their geo-political context. It also emphasises the urgency for nuanced, conversation-based impact assessment in development studies, moving beyond quantitative metrics. The chapter concludes by offering a glimpse into the multifaceted realities captured in the ensuing ethnographies thus contributing to the interdisciplinary discourse of development.

Keywords COVID-19 pandemic · Feminist ethnography · Informal workers · Vulnerable communities · Gender disparities · Socio-economic complexities

1 I

Life in the post-pandemic world is like looking into a glasshouse of insufficient and mangled web of complex systems. The fragility of institutions and systemic processes in the face of a global shutdown has since caused stakeholders to question the foundations on which the world functions in the twenty-first century—alliances, power hierarchies, and information dissemination. Previously invisible, or deliberately ignored issues, such as inefficient infrastructure capabilities, underfunded and collapsing healthcare systems, and inequitable access to resources were forcibly brought to light (Laboul et al., 2021; Ferreira, 2021; WHO Interim Report, 2022). The COVID-19 pandemic has served as a litmus test, revealing both the adaptability of existing frameworks, the resilience of socio-economic paradigms, and global governance structures, prompting a critical reevaluation of their effectiveness and preparedness for future challenges.

Governments all over the globe channelised and mobilised the majority of their fiscal resources towards mitigating the adverse socio-economic effects surfacing from the pandemic. As excess mortality increased from 3 million in 2020 to around 15 million in 2021, countries adopted all forms of counter-measures to get their receding economies back on track (United Nations Department of Economic and Social Affairs [UNDESA], n.d.; World Health Organisation [WHO], n.d.). As per the Oxford COVID-19 Government Response Tracker's (OxCGRT) Stringency Index, some nations implemented relatively regimented regulations that restricted movement for an individual for anything apart from essential work. Meanwhile, some others opted for a more libertarian approach, allowing more mobility and access to the commons (Hale et al., 2021).

The second wave of the COVID-19 health crisis (March 2021–June 2021) brought more academic and media attention and scrutiny to developing nations like India and how we handled the shock across states. The primary stirring effect arose from the striking visuals which were constantly displayed to the nation—families outside hospitals crying for a bed, mothers begging for oxygen tanks to save their children, and piles of bodies burnt. This distress documented, in conjunction with inequalities persisting in India, sought revaluation of regulations and policies, and perhaps even the very foundations on which the nation was built post-independence (Kugler & Sinh, 2020). Over time, as these systemic failures were highlighted, it became increasingly evident that the challenges were not transient in nature but deeply rooted in the nation's fabric. The prolonged crisis has underscored the urgency for an inward-looking approach, involving comprehensive reforms and innovations not only to address immediate concerns but also to build a more resilient and inclusive future for the country.

Amidst the harrowing visuals and systemic breakdowns observed during the COVID-19 crisis, it is essential to delve further into the enduring disparities that have long moulded India's social, economic, and political terrain. Across India's diverse topographies and demographics, it was the marginalised communities occupying informal spaces[1] that were put at a graver risk than others. This was a symptom of an identity-based hierarchical system that relegates vulnerable individuals to unfair treatment and exclusion. While the crisis was at the forefront of all decision-making processes, the precariousness in the lives of such groups residing on the fringes persisted, especially in the lived tale of those working in the most unsecured sectors of the economy. Social scientists

[1] Based on Lutzoni's (2016) conception, informal spaces are as invisibilised communal spaces occupied by people of similar caste, class, and a shared uncertainty in labour, living, and social conditions. This has been defined extensively in Chapter 2: (Feminist) Ethnography in Crisis.

often try to study the governing dynamics of informality from perspectives of legality and illegality (in defining what's formal and informal). However, there are several other dimensions and applications of its presence as an experienced reality for millions of workers in India.

Narratives evolving from marginalised communities revealed the impact of "othering" and the systemic exclusion they faced. Initially conceptualised by Gayatri Spivak (1985) to represent the distinction between the colonised and the colonisers, the notion of "othering" has since expanded to encompass those in the lower socio-economic strata in the post-colonial world. These individuals, already burdened by issues such as resource inaccessibility, underpayment, and overwork, faced additional challenges during the pandemic. While some found solace in their homes during the sudden lockdown, the "others" were given minimal notice to return to their hometowns, enduring arduous journeys amidst tumultuous conditions. A part of the "other", members of the informal workforce,[2] were forced to toil away for gruelling hours without receiving fair compensation and benefits for their labour through the health crisis (Murthy, 2019).

Amidst the broader context of communities grappling with the manifold challenges wrought by the pandemic, a distinct narrative emerged concerning the pronounced vulnerabilities experienced by women in India—"others" within the "others". The complex interplay of deeply entrenched gender-based roles and responsibilities inherent in the Indian society rendered women particularly susceptible to the pandemic's adverse impacts. The preexisting structural inequities were glaring, with a substantial proportion of women primarily engaged in the informal sector. Paradoxically, their invaluable contributions in the realm of domestic labour, while sustaining households and communities, remained unaccounted for in the national Gross Domestic Product (GDP). This resulted in the invisibilisation of their labour and an enduring alienation from the formal workforce. The onset of the pandemic exacerbated these challenges further, necessitating women to adeptly navigate the intricate web

[2] Informal workforce comprises people who fall outside the purview of formal economic structures and their contributions are not accounted for in official statistics. These include those outside formal employment, often due to factors like limited education, lack of skills, and other socio-economic factors such as caste, in the case of India. More often than not, these roles are characterised by inter-generational skills that are not taught in the formal training systems available in the country (Basole 2014, p. 10; Deléchat and Medina 2020; Gammarano and Kapsos 2018; Sheikh and Gaurav 2020).

of household chores while simultaneously engaging in their indispensable but often unrecognised informal labour.

Notably, this multifaceted burden was compounded by the conspicuous absence of support mechanisms to alleviate the strains. The alarming surge in cases of intimate partner violence, a tormenting consequence of prolonged confinement and heightened tensions, underscored the critical need for protective measures. Daughters-in-law also recounted experiencing violence perpetrated by other members of the family. The situation deteriorated to such an extent that statistical data uncovered an exponential increase in the volume of online reports of domestic violence filed by women. This upswing exceeded the records by four times in a comparable timeframe over the preceding decade, as indicated by the reports of multiple women advocacy groups in India (Office of the United Nations High Commissioner for Human Rights, 2022). However, this data only partially reflects the distressing reality, as numerous cases remain unreported due to the persisting stigma surrounding domestic abuse within the Indian society. The extent of the situation can only be surmised and calls for urgent concern. This multifaceted landscape reflects the apparent gender disparities exacerbated by the pandemic, underlining the imperative for a nuanced and comprehensive analysis of the disproportionate adversities.

Spanning across two years, each narrative identified in this edited anthology will capture the pandemic's effects on the vulnerable workforce at different points in time, aiming to study how the crisis affected their lives-livelihoods and what coping mechanisms each identified worker group developed to respond to the shock. This volume is a culmination of several feminist ethnographic research projects undertaken by the Centre for New Economics Studies (CNES) that unpack and analyse the disproportionate impact of the COVID-19 shock on "informal" workers across varied spatial sensibilities. Ranging from fisherfolk to steel manufacturers, waste pickers to sanitation workers, people who were at the forefront of providing sustenance struggled to sustain themselves.

The attempt to capture the stories of these vulnerable communities in a holistic manner, without sensationalising their hardships, posed several challenging questions: *Why is doing research in grim times necessary? What methodology is most effective in the production and mobilisation of knowledge?* To seek answers to some of these questions and capture ground realities, our research team, involving multiple ethnographers and contributors, engaged in fieldwork. We used an audio-visual format of archiving interviews and adopted a feminist ethnographic approach to studying the effects of the crisis on the workforce across cities in India.

Chapter 2, which details the methodology, documents our efforts to avoid the oversimplification of complex narratives into one-dimensional representations, especially when dealing with vulnerable communities living in informal spaces. The use of semi-structured interviews and participant observations provided a unique space for respondents to express their stories on their own terms. Recognising that no single approach can capture the full spectrum of lived experiences, we navigated the field with a mix of quantitative and qualitative methodologies that embraced a wide range of voices. This helped in ensuring that we heard as many perspectives as possible, ultimately providing a comprehensive representation of the community's multidimensional experiences. The narrative approach, underpinned by feminist ethnography, also ensured that the voices of the researched community were at the forefront.

This feminist perspective underlined the persisting power hierarchies and imbalances that often permeate ethnographic research. Various tenets of pedagogy, such as self-reflexivity and collaboration, encouraged us, the researchers, to place ourselves in the shoes of those marginalised within society, thereby fostering a deeper understanding of their realities. The ethos of adaptability also formed the cornerstone of the team's inquiry as we constantly consulted different participants in the study to ensure the co-production of a collective rhetoric. Furthermore, involving the community itself in the research process served to dismantle barriers to information and foster a collaborative spirit. By scrutinising the roadblocks to exercising women's agency, feminist ethnography enriched our comprehension of multifaceted issues while actively working to reshape the boundaries of knowledge production.

In conversation with our field ethnographers, we also reflected on the challenges faced by them when dealing with communities wary of "outsiders", grappling with the complexities of their social identities, and navigating the fine balance between power dynamics in fieldwork. Despite this, the field ethnographers stressed the significance of sidestepping a singular narrative and recognised the importance of narratives that embrace the diversity and nuance of the communities studied. Our goal, therefore, is to present the overlooked experiences authentically and comprehensively while remaining attuned to the social and cultural stratification that influences their lives.

2 II

The (feminist) ethnographies of crisis discussed in this anthology present a myriad of realities co-existing simultaneously in informal spaces. Since our research scope was determined by the geographical location of the lead field researcher at the time, we had the capability to integrate socio-spatio-temporal diversity into the discourse. This section, therefore, presents a broad overview of the carefully curated case studies recorded in this edited book.

2.1 *Navigating Through Shocks:* Mīṉavar *of Tamil Nadu and Puducherry*

This chapter is a culmination of ethnographic research that was conducted on fisherfolk in parts of Tamil Nadu and Puducherry during the two-month annual ban period (April–June), offering a unique vantage point for an in-depth examination. Employing a feminist ethnographic lens, the researchers engaged in semi-structured interviews and participant observations, skilfully navigating the complexities and power dynamics inherent in the research process. The responses capture the nuances of the lives and livelihoods of this community, as they juggled a hectic work schedule with constant and recurring shocks. The team established rapport with the community, surmounting obstacles such as language barriers and cultural nuances, thus securing the trust of the participants. These coastal inhabitants grapple with a plethora of challenges, ranging from unpredictable environmental hazards to economic constraints and the scarcity of essential infrastructural resources.

The study meticulously dissects the nuanced elements embedded within the lives of fisherfolk, illuminating their daily realities and the intricate socio-economic complexities that define their lives. This exploration builds on the "multiple dimensions of well-being in practice" framework, as introduced by Coulthard et al. (2018), scrutinising the economic, social, and environmental circumstances that envelop these communities. This has also aided in dismantling some preconceived notions about the fishers in the region and bringing forward their diverse personal histories and rhetorics.

Gender polarities, money management, and youth participation and their effects on the continuity of trade have been explored. An analysis of their spending choices, elucidated through the paradigm of "poor economics" by Banerjee and Duflo, reveals intriguing trade-offs. However, the socio-economic networks of these fishing communities are not solely delineated by economic transactions, but also intricately woven with gender dynamics. Women, despite their often-overlooked roles, assume pivotal responsibilities in managing household finances, while the men predominantly steer the financial decisions concerning fishing. Youth participation in a trade, which is considered a traditional vocation, faces a palpable decline as the younger generation gravitates towards alternate livelihoods.

Additionally, this chapter delves into assessing the influence of the transition to a new epoch, the Anthropocene, and rampant marine pollution on fishers and the trade at large. Finally, the research juxtaposes the 2004 Tsunami with the 2020 COVID-19 pandemic to assess temporal vulnerabilities and discusses the requirement for ex-post and preventive policy measures to deal with shocks. Overall, this comprehensive exploration offers a profound insight into the intricate fabric of fisherfolk's lives, shedding light on their social, economic, and gender complexities, thereby contributing to a holistic understanding of this community.

2.2 *Flooding Urbanity: Narratives from* Safai Karamcharis *of Guwahati, Assam*

Post the devastating floods of Assam in 2022, a team of ethnographers took to the streets of the capital city, Guwahati, to explore the turbulent hydro-social dynamics. In the midst of the city's bustling life, sanitation workers, known as *safai karamcharis*, persevered regardless of inclement weather. This chapter is a documentation of the hidden narrative of sanitation workers in the slums of Guwahati, a community doomed to cater to the needs of the urban collective over their own. Even during the most severe floods, these individuals depend on completing tasks for their income. Despite their pivotal role in maintaining public health, these labourers endure job dissatisfaction and financial insecurity. More often than not, they are underpaid and burdened with the perception of menial labour.

Through a combination of in-depth interviews and focus groups, the researchers gathered data, considering the unique social and environmental context. The research team's dynamic positionality, influenced by their varied social identities, played a significant role in building rapport with the community and finding informants. The feminist ethnographic methodology used highlighted the intersectionality of caste, class, and gender in the lives of sanitation workers in Guwahati, emphasising the need to understand and address their vulnerabilities and challenges within the broader socio-ecological context.

By compiling the responses, the chapter delves into the nuances of caste and gender dimensions that govern the fragile livelihoods of the community most vulnerable to floods in the region—*safai karamcharis*. Stranded at the bottom rung of society, they are forced to navigate their lives with scant resources and limited government support. During floods, their restricted access to amenities worsens drainage blockages and rising water levels, creating a detrimental cycle. The burden disproportionately affects female sanitation workers. Belonging to lower-caste backgrounds, they continue to work during floods, often living in cramped conditions.

The study explores the undertones of informality in a formal work set-up and the cyclical nature of annual flooding. The work of sanitation personnel blurs the boundary between formal and informal labour, rendering it a neglected concern in employment and livelihood policies. Struggling with unfair wage deductions and additional uncontracted duties, they encounter an acute shortage of proper equipment. Floods further aggravate the gender divide, with women forced to travel longer distances and shoulder additional responsibilities. Gendered expectations necessitate that they fulfil numerous household roles, including the procurement of clean water, often balancing heavy loads. Unrelenting in their dedication, these women rarely have time for self-care, enduring heightened vulnerability to gender-based violence during disasters.

The observations and analysis from this project add to Coulthard et al.'s (2018) concept of Multidimensionality of Poverty. The research expanded the definition of "ecosystem services" to include sanitation work, recognising the importance of these workers in maintaining the urban ecosystem's well-being, especially during a crisis. In conclusion, the hardships plaguing *safai karamcharis* remain a blight on society, and their struggles during flooding underscore the urgent need for improved policies and support for these essential workers.

2.3 Living Among Waste: *Bachaikaris* of Bhalswa

This chapter is a feminist ethnographic inquiry into an often-overlooked community of waste pickers, dwelling on the fringes of urban existence within the Bhalswa region of Delhi, India. Also known as *Bachaikaris*, these resilient individuals migrated from West Bengal and are instrumental in managing the legacy waste amassed at the landfill. Therefore, their lived experiences warrant a deep dive-in. This study endeavours to amplify the voices of waste pickers and expose the gendered dimensions of their struggles for recognition and dignity. Discrimination and marginalisation endure as these labourers bear the burden of societal perceptions that assign them to the lowest rungs of the caste hierarchy. At the heart of this investigation lies the intricate interplay of caste dynamics, gender inequities, and the involvement of children in this sector. Feminist ethnography, in this context, serves as a powerful tool to unearth the gendered and caste nuances of their daily lives.

In the Bhalswa vicinity, waste pickers additionally confront an array of challenges relating to labour conditions, citizenship, and the profound consequences of the COVID-19 pandemic. The privatisation of waste management has pushed their livelihoods into further precarity, making them even more vulnerable to exploitation. This research unpacks the layers of these challenges, spotlighting the power dynamics at play. Moreover, this study presents a resounding call to action, advocating for the recognition of waste pickers as indispensable actors within the broader waste management landscape. Building from a holistic understanding of their lived experiences, this chapter analyses the need for safeguarding the dignity, rights, and livelihoods of the marginalised *Bachaikaris*. Therefore, the underlying theme is to foster a more equitable and inclusive approach to waste management.

2.4 *Cycle of Poverty: Analysing the Social Structures of the Women of Kapashera*

In the context of India's rapid urbanisation and economic growth, the emergence of slum-like areas such as Kapashera has become increasingly prevalent, serving as a stark illustration of the everyday challenges encountered by low-income rural–urban migrants. This chapter delves into the intricate social structures that contribute to the perpetuation of poverty and gender disparities within the migrant community of Kapashera, a dilapidating industrial area situated on the border of Delhi and Haryana.

Adopting a feminist ethnographic approach, this study takes a nuanced perspective on the lives of the women in Kapashera, emphasising their central roles within the community. These women not only provide crucial domestic support to their families but also navigate the socio-economic constraints imposed by traditional gender roles. The limited visibility and agency stemming from these norms presented a significant hurdle in the process of data collection. Nevertheless, the research team identified intersections of gender, education, health, and daily wage labour and connected the observations to Jan Breman's (1999) ideas of freedom and bondage.

The geographical isolation of these slums further compounds the challenges faced in obtaining essential services and employment opportunities, thereby fuelling a vicious cycle of poverty. The research explores the influence of external factors, including government policies, economic fluctuations, and the disruptive impact of the COVID-19 pandemic on the already precarious livelihoods of migrant women in Kapashera. The research also identifies challenges to unionisation, which would otherwise significantly improve the lives of women in the region.

The chapter, thus, offers a critical exploration of gender inequalities, social structures, and the increasing casualisation of labour in low-income urban settlements. It underscores the urgent need to document and amplify the worker's experiences in order to address the specific hardships they endure. Ultimately, the study reveals the urgent requirement for interventions that take into account the intricate realities of these women's lives, transcending mere observation to facilitate meaningful change.

3 III

This edited anthology of research projects aims to amplify the experiences and vulnerabilities of marginalised, and unsecured worker communities by sharing stories from various corners of India. As editors of the volume, our effort through this book is also to encourage a more interactive approach to analysing and unpacking myriad developmental landscapes. We emphasise the significance of comprehending the lives, livelihoods, and circumstances of the "others", which is often overlooked in mainstream data collection exercises. We advocate for approaches that extend beyond mere quantitative metrics, placing value on a more expansive, conversation-based outlook within the realms of impact assessment and development studies, especially across the growing informal sector.

You will find each chapter to be arranged in a similar pattern to how we conduct our research—context and conversation, followed by reflection.

Each of the aforementioned case studies features in-depth individual interviews with the field ethnographers on the methodology and perspectives. We further cross-analyse their ideas with our understanding, notions, and dilemmas associated with (feminist) ethnographic projects. This, we believe, is an alternate way to disseminate research analysis, which brings a reader closer to the community whom we have co-produced the narratives with. In doing so, we hope to encourage interdisciplinary applications that enhance our understanding of these complex issues and add to the discourse.

References

Basole, A. (2014, October). The Informal Sector from a Knowledge Perspective. *Down to Earth, Yojana(Loka-Vidya), 58*, 8–13.

Breman, J. (1999). The Study of Industrial Labour in Post-Colonial India—The Formal Sector: An Introductory Review. *Contributions to Indian Sociology, 33*(1–2), 1–41. https://doi.org/10.1177/006996679903300104

Coulthard, S., Mcgregor, J. A., & White, C. S. (2018). Chapter 15: Multiple Dimensions of Wellbeing in Practice. In K. Schreckenberg, G. Mace, & M. Poudyal (Eds.), *Ecosystem Services and Poverty Alleviation: Trade-offs and Governance* (pp. 243–256). Routledge.

Deléchat, C., & Medina, L. (2020, December). *What is the Informal Economy?* International Monetary Fund. https://www.imf.org/en/Publications/fandd/issues/2020/12/what-is-the-informal-economy-basics

Ferreira, F. (2021). *Inequality and COVID-19* [Finance & Development]. International Monetary Fund. https://www.imf.org/external/pubs/ft/fandd/2021/06/pdf/inequality-and-covid-19-ferreira.pdf

Gammarano, R., & Kapsos, S. (2018). *Decent Work and the Sustainable Development Goals: A Guidebook on SDG Labour Market Indicators*. International Labour Organization.

Hale, T., Angrist, N., Goldszmidt, R., Kira, B., Petherick, A., Phillips, T., Webster, S., Cameron-Blake, E., Hallas, L., Majumdar, S., & Tatlow, H. (2021). A Global Panel Database of Pandemic Policies (Oxford COVID-19 Government Response Tracker). *Nature Human Behaviour*, *5*(4), Article 4. https://doi.org/10.1038/s41562-021-01079-8

Kugler, M., & Sinha, S. (2020, July 13). The Impact of COVID-19 and the Policy Response in India. *Brookings*. https://www.brookings.edu/blog/future-development/2020/07/13/the-impact-of-covid-19-and-the-policy-response-in-india/

Laboul, A., Bishop, T., & Paula, J. (2021). *COVID-19 and a New Resilient Infrastructure Landscape* (Tackling Coronavirus (COVID-19)). Organisation for Economic Co-operation and Development (OECD). https://read.oecd-ilibrary.org/view/?ref=1060_1060483-4roq9lf7eu&title=COVID-19-and-a-new-resilient-infrastructure-landscape

Lutzoni, L. (2016). In-formalised Urban Space Design. Rethinking the Relationship Between Formal and Informal. *City, Territory and Architecture*, *3*(1), 20. https://doi.org/10.1186/s40410-016-0046-9

Murthy, S. V. R. (2019, November 14). Measuring Informal Economy in India. *Session II: Traditional Estimation Practices: Determining the Level and Growth of the Informal Economy.* 7th IMF Statistical Forum: Measuring the Informal Economy. https://www.imf.org/en/News/Seminars/Conferences/2019/03/25/7th-statistical-forum

Office of the United Nations High Commissioner for Human Rights (2022). *COVID-19 and the Increase of Domestic Violence against Women.* https://www.ohchr.org/sites/default/files/2022-01/india-womens-r-network.pdf

Sheikh, R. A., & Gaurav, S. (2020). Informal Work in India: A Tale of Two Definitions. *The European Journal of Development Research, 32*(4), 1105–1127. https://doi.org/10.1057/s41287-020-00258-z

Spivak, G. C. (1985). The Rani of Sirmur: An Essay in Reading the Archives. *History and Theory, 24*(3), 247–272. https://doi.org/10.2307/2505169

United Nations Department of Economic and Social Affairs. (n.d.). *14.9 Million Excess Deaths Associated with the COVID-19 Pandemic in 2020 and 2021.* United Nations. Retrieved June 23, 2023, from https://www.un.org/en/desa/149-million-excess-deaths-associated-covid-19-pandemic-2020-and-2021

World Health Organisation. (n.d.). *The True Death Toll of COVID-19: Estimating Global Excess Mortality.* Retrieved June 23, 2023, from https://www.who.int/data/stories/the-true-death-toll-of-covid-19-estimating-global-excess-mortality

World Health Organization (2022). *Third Round of the Global Pulse Survey on Continuity of Essential Health Services During the COVID-19 Pandemic* [Interim Report]. https://www.who.int/publications-detail-redirect/WHO-2019-nCoV-EHS_continuity-survey-2022.1

CHAPTER 2

[Feminist] Ethnography in Crisis

Sakshi Chindaliya, Ashika Thomas, Deepanshu Mohan, and Arun Kumar Kaushik

Abstract This chapter explores the challenges and adaptations in ethnographic research conducted in informal spaces during the COVID-19 pandemic in India. The chapter explores methodological tools unique to ethnography practices and the changes it underwent due to the

S. Chindaliya (✉) · D. Mohan · A. K. Kaushik
Jindal School of Liberal Arts and Humanities, O.P. Jindal Global University, Sonipat, India
e-mail: sakshichindaliya@yahoo.in

D. Mohan
e-mail: dmohan@jgu.edu.in

A. K. Kaushik
e-mail: akkaushik@jgu.edu.in

D. Mohan
Centre for New Economics Studies, Jindal School of Liberal Arts And Humanities, Jindal Global University, Sonipat, O.P, India

A. Thomas
London School of Economics and Political Science, London, UK
e-mail: ashikathms@gmail.com

D. Mohan et al. (eds.), *Pan-India Stories of Informal Workers During Covid-19 Pandemic*, https://doi.org/10.1007/978-981-97-1525-1_2

restricted conditions during lockdowns. The pandemic disrupted traditional long-term engagements, compelling researchers to rely on brief interactions, digital ethnography, and sparse interactions during fieldwork. The chapter details the complexities of fieldwork in informal spaces, addressing scepticism from respondents and ethical dilemmas amidst global crises. The methodology incorporates feminist ethnography, aiming to capture diverse voices and avoid oversimplification among vulnerabilities. In addition to this, the chapter explores specific tools under feminist ethnography including (self-)reflexivity, polyvocality, and collaboration which aided the authors in presenting a nuanced understanding of vulnerable communities' experiences. The authors advocate for a pluralistic narrative approach to convey the multifaceted realities of informal spaces during the pandemic, providing insights for policymakers and civil servants aiming to impact grassroots levels.

Keywords Ethnographic research · COVID-19 pandemic · Informal spaces · Feminist ethnography · Narrative approach · Polyvocality · Collaboration

At the beginning of the pandemic, when mobility was limited and people outside were sparse, Jignesh Mistry, a photojournalist, took the opportunity to interact with those who had no choice but to stay out of their homes to work. This observation made in Pune, Mistry's hometown, was also noted in Lucknow by a resident research assistant. This led to the creation of a narrative project based on interactions with similar communities closest to the homes of the research team. Most studies explored in this anthology are chance encounters, pockets of narratives that were stumbled upon while travelling through and occupying time and space. What carried the projects forward was a mixture of general interest and a lack of predisposed knowledge of the community among the researchers. This allowed us to be inducted into the field, genuinely curious about the "local interpretations" of the locals themselves (Fetterman, 2010; Geertz, 1973). To engage with the ground realities, we resorted to using ethnography, a method of documenting the culture and experiences of a community. By situating ourselves in the informant's habitus, we were able to observe and participate in unpacking socio-cultural nuance, "choice" making, and interpersonal dynamics. Borrowing from Spradley and McCurdy (2012) definition of ethnography, as understanding "how the members of a particular community see their world", we found ourselves employing it to not only understand their mundane but their response to the global health crisis.

Time proved to be simultaneously the most frustrating and rewarding tenant of our ethnographic projects. In a "normal" setting, before the pandemic, we could depend on long-term, sustained engagement to build trust with the respondents, and give them room to narrate their stories the way they choose to, without inhibitions (Hosokawa, 2010, p. 5, cited in Hamal, 2020, p. 1). The pandemic, however, took away this traditional aspect of long-term fieldwork, replacing it with brief interactions during which we had to capture the whole essence of what would otherwise be a months-long, if not years-long, project. As opposed to the deductive nature of the research we had undertaken before, where we based our approach on pre-existing concepts, the pandemic forced us to tackle new problems. While we had certain points of contact who helped us build and navigate the complex socio-cultural ecosystems, there were several respondents we encountered on the field whom we could not trace our steps back to. Stifled with uncertainty, a linear data collection process proved to be almost impossible, as there were breaks in previously seen patterns and trends.

Another methodology that gained traction during the pandemic was "digital ethnography". Researchers began collecting data online, utilising digital spaces as their "field" to conduct their inquiry. However, more often than not, the demographic that we were working with did not have the infrastructural capabilities to connect on online platforms like Zoom, Google Meet or Microsoft Teams. Let alone video conferencing software, most respondents that we interviewed could not afford to buy smartphones or find a stable channel to connect via a network call. Considering the expensive data costs, they only had limited access to the internet. The digital divide persistent in India alienated the invisibilised communities yet again. Therefore, for us, digital ethnography did not seem like a viable option.

Ultimately, physical research was heavily localised to the researchers present in different parts of India. While some of us ethnographers were present on the field, most of us were confined to our own homes. Ideation took place over Zoom meetings and observations in the short trips out of home, made to get essentials. Meanwhile, fieldwork was, as authors Gökçe Günel et al. (2020) put it, "patchy" with discernable differences between field and home. Visual cues, such as candid pictures and video recordings of people, their work and their surroundings, aided the team in weaving a narrative based on various stories by giving faces to names. These later became an important part of the narrative itself, enabling anyone to visualise a pandemic experience different to their own and to identify nuance often lost through words. The pandemic, thus, meant being reliant on field notes, recorded interviews and visuals from the field, and post-visit online discussions.

While we were able to figure out ways to continue ethnographic research during lockdowns, we faced other roadblocks. More often than not, we were faced with valid and challenging questions from the respondents:

Why should we speak to you?
How is this productive for us?
We could be working instead of answering your questions.

Almost like clockwork, most interactions would begin with such scepticism. The informants' hesitancy extended beyond a mere reluctance to share personal narratives; their perplexity stemmed from questioning the relevance of inquiring about their monthly financial data amidst a global crisis of unprecedented proportions. Over the last two years and across various geographies, the diverse group of ethnographers in this anthology echoed this ethical dilemma. With the ever-increasing mortality rate and the collective feeling of loss amidst the furore of the pandemic, we pondered over the "bigger picture". *Why undergo such an elongated process of documenting narratives amidst the rapid pace of the coronavirus taking the world by storm? At a time and space when finding immediate solutions was at the forefront of every conversation, how were our research projects placed when the ability to render instantaneous relief to problems identified was uncertain? Do we have the means to build a symbiotic relationship with the respondents, or are these interactions beneficial solely to us?*

A part of our research journey was to sit in discomfort, knowing that we did not have access to resources for providing such immediate relief or solutions. In our process of (un)learning, we had to constantly remind ourselves that while we may not have concrete or convincing responses to these questions, we research and write in the hope of archiving their grievances and addressing issues at a systemic level. While reflecting on short-term policies and corroborating them with on-ground evidence, we found that the current format of assessing lives and livelihood does not adequately capture the reality of marginalised communities. The existing set of methods used to study these groups for policy-making purposes limits the respondent's experiences to quantifiable entities, simplifying the same (Ahmed, 2006; Avishai et al., 2013; Crawley, 2012; Denzin, 2014, as cited in Heath et al., 2022, p. 11). However, statistics and numbers only capture the interest of political leaders and the privileged in positions of power, who prefer that to the instability of emotions conveyed through community narratives (Davis & Craven, 2016). Hence, the idea was to contextualise their circumstances in the larger scheme of socio-economic and cultural stratification.

1 Informal Spaces and the Narrative Approach

For a more holistic perspective and also to make the material appealing to those hyper-fixated on "numbers", we resorted to more mixed methodological models. At the onset of the pandemic, Jignesh Mistry and the team perceived the sudden hypervisibility of vulnerable communities in informal spaces. Based on our visits, building onto Lutzoni's (2016) conception, we identified informal spaces as invisibilised communal spaces occupied by people of similar caste, class, and a shared uncertainty in labour, living and social conditions. They fall outside the purview of normative frameworks of work and are not governed by any institutional mechanisms, ultimately becoming a blind spot for government and policymakers alike. Co-existing alongside formal spaces, informality is a function of "othering", i.e. the exclusion of certain communities from the mainstream rhetoric. While Spivak's (1985) initial theorisation of "othering" was intended to portray the exclusion of the colonised from the colonisers, it has now expanded to reflect the nuances of the postcolonial world. The "others" today are people who occupy the lower rungs of the socio-economic hierarchies and are forced to find home in the fringes of urban spaces. Even in cases where they are present (and very much visible) at the heart of cities, they are often neglected and their neighbourhoods are deemed as unclean. During the pandemic, people from informal spaces were still battling the pre-existing set of issues, such as inaccessibility to resources and their underpaid and overworked status, that plagued them. The groups that were already afflicted with uncertainties had an added layer of burden looming over them.

At the offset of the pandemic, when the sudden lockdown was announced in India, some, despite battling the anxiety of what was to come, retreated to the comfort of their own homes. Meanwhile, the "others" were given less than 24 hours' notice to pack their lives and march back to their hometowns. The horrid images of workers feebly making their way back home in the intolerable heat were circulated widely across various media platforms (Basu, 2020; Siddiqui, 2020; *The Indian Express*, 2020). With the informal spaces still bustling with movement, the intersectional identities of some placed the others in a graver position, exacerbating the challenges and disadvantages they were faced with. Expectations within informal spaces are different, as rules and norms applicable elsewhere in society are considered malleable to suit one's immediate needs of survival. While authors Shaw and Hudson (2009) find this "soft malleability" to provide a safe haven from public spaces (where they are ridiculed), we found that it promotes uncertainty and exploitation of labour terms. Amidst the grim circumstances, we had a chance to unpack the layered experiences of the historicities and current lives of vulnerable informal communities.

As an ethnographer on the field, handling interactions in informal spaces is challenging in many ways as it is riddled with a multitude of interrelated socio-political and cultural divides. Here, one can encounter a complex interplay between civil law and held human beliefs, between opposing faiths and codependency, and, particularly in the context of the pandemic, a fragile line between survival and starvation. These nuanced interactions coexist amidst the backdrop of dilapidated structures found in migrant colonies and other informal settlements. These spaces, often regarded as microcosms of social inequalities, defy simplistic classification and challenge the conventional dichotomous notion of their existence and dynamics. Rather than fitting neatly into a binary framework, these interactions resemble more of a metaphorical web, symbolising the intricate networks of social classification at play. Thus, it becomes imperative not to exclude this complexity from the data collection process, as doing so would perpetuate the flawed duality in our perception of urban populations.

Dani Rodrik (2023), in his recent piece, *On Productivism,* elaborates upon this dualism trap that the development discourse in the current times has fallen into. In the gap between rich and poor, formal and informal work, lies a huge demographic, unnoticed in policy spheres and academia—the diversity of which has not been studied enough. The high variability in the landscape requires a more nuanced comprehension to provide an "accurate" representation of these diverse demographics. Where sole reliance on quantitative methodologies cannot hold a mirror to the heterogeneity within these seemingly homogeneous groups, a narrative approach can help in documenting the myriad of co-existing (and perhaps conflicting) realities in these spaces. Singular accounts are misleading, labelling communities as just "poor" or just "artisanal". As we moved from studying invisibilised economic sectors, such as the Tamil fishing industry, to invisibilised populations, such as the residents of settler colonies, we aimed to pull away from the existing binaries associated with these systems.

We realised a way to achieve this was to collect and put together multiple voices, helping us depict not just the extremes but the in-betweens. Giving them the voice to communicate the issues they believe to be important during all interactions ensured that the respondents had the agency to identify the issues that plague them and articulate their needs. In a serendipitous discovery, we soon found means to best encapsulate the multiplicity in experiences by using the feminist ethnographic framework. Feminist ethnographers not only approach the field with a gendered perspective but also focus on other forms of social stratification, such as class, caste, and race (Davis & Craven, 2016; Ghosh, 2016). Alongside acknowledging the socio-cultural context, we also document infrastructure capabilities and engage in mapping their broader historical trajectories to help readers visualise the current dynamics better. While this shift in methodology is not recent by any means, an ardent need for this alternate way of approaching a community became more pertinent at the onset of the pandemic. As the world went into lockdown, ethnographic methods had to adapt (Günel et al., 2020; Lems, 2020; Sumesh & Gogoi, 2021).

Among others, it was a challenge to communicate with members of communities without fear of the virus. In a time when these folks were living in trepidation of unemployment and destitution, asking scheduled questions from a clear position of privilege had put us in tricky situations. The restriction on mobility added challenges and led to more scrutiny on law enforcers' behalf. This meant that the research team had to find appropriate means to interact with the respondents in their natural habitats, pick on visual and behavioural cues, map body language and effectively source information for the studies. In lieu of the circumstances faced by us, shifting to a feminist ethnographic model of conducting field studies seemed more suitable. This transition in approaching research with more nuance was achieved by incorporating audio-visual cues in documenting stories. The discourse evolving from such visual documentation not only provided a long-standing memory but also put the onus of directing the narrative on the respondents. It left room for a wide-ranging interpretation of the stories being told and created avenues for comparisons in the future.

2 Feminist Ethnography in Practice

While feminist ethnography is a research approach rooted in exploring perspectives of women while challenging and deconstructing traditional male-centred narratives, the case studies explored in this anthology also focus on questions outside the realm of the gendered lens. We employed tenants of feminist ideologies to the ethnographic methodological framework to uncover the often hidden or marginalised stories and to provide a more comprehensive understanding of the "others'" roles, struggles, and agency within the Indian context. By exploring men's experiences within the framework of feminist ethnography, we had the opportunity to delve into how gender and power dynamics are constructed, negotiated, and performed at work as well as at home. Ultimately, as Sandra Harding (1987) argues, feminist ethnography has the capacity to challenge and deconstruct conventional gender binaries, offering a more nuanced exploration of power, identity, and social dynamics.

Our reliance on epistemological perspectives that view knowledge as a dynamic interaction between those acquiring knowledge and the subjects of that knowledge helped us to effectively co-produce narratives with the research subjects. To stay true to the core value of feminist ethnography—collaboration—not only was the discourse development done alongside the community being researched upon, but each step of the research cycle was executed in cahoots with a research team (Benson & Nagar, 2006; Davis & Craven, 2016; Ghosh, 2016). Scholars hailing from different demographics, geographies, and disciplinary backgrounds came together to design the study and build knowledge networks with experts (both academic and otherwise). We were able to establish an input mechanism to facilitate this conversation. Consequently, the data documenting, processing and analysis were also done in solidarity with the diverse research design team to ensure the myriad interdisciplinary realities were well-captured and articulated.

Apart from internal collaboration, the co-production of knowledge with community members who were convinced about not engaging with government officials or journalists proved to be challenging. They often cited stories of unkept promises and betrayed trust, as such groups had misused the information shared, which pushed these vulnerable communities into dismay and further precarity. While tending to their hesitations, our primary goal was to clarify our purpose of entering their space and requesting their time. We could visibly see the informants allay their doubts as they found out that we were a research team (mostly students) from a university. However, that was just the first milestone we crossed, anticipating many others until we reached the end. The next was to garner their interest and engage in a meaningful conversation. This dialogue was centred around us being there to simply listen and emphasise the importance of their voice. As difficult as it was, we were rewarded with their trust and candour, allowing efficient collaboration with the respondents.

To effectively negotiate the agency between the interviewer and the interviewee, we used semi-structured interviews, in conjunction with participant observations, to provide different respondents with the space to tell their stories the way they wanted to. Even within groups commonly marked as a homogeneous entity, we found that diverse, and sometimes conflicting, narratives emerged from our interaction. Building on these varied personal accounts, we used the practice of polyvocality, under the ambit of feminist ethnography, to critically analyse the points of convergence and divergence from these interviews, adding nuance to the emerging discourse. Polyvocality also helped us escape the issue of painting a layman's image of a vulnerable group by imbibing a multitude of experiences from a community with a similar socio-economic and cultural background (Davis & Craven, 2016). Together, collaboration and polyvocality provided us with room for this nexus of co-production of knowledge to exist. While the former shared their individual histories and lived experiences, we could use theoretical models to place these (non)discernable patterns in the overarching paradigm (Arksey & Knight, 1999).

Another thing we tried to be vary of was to constantly question our preconceived notions and avoid the minimisation of interviewee's experiences to their alleged cultural inferiority. Especially as we entered the field as "outsiders" [or "partial insiders" in some studies], we had to be very conscious of the social stratification in the Indian context (Ghosh, 2016). The term "partial insiders" has been used here deliberately and with caution. We visualised the complex interplay of social identities as a unique Venn diagram wherein the intersectional identities of the researcher and the respondent overlapped at some points and diverged at others. Socialisation, learning the performance of different identity markers, has taught us what aspect of our simultaneous and co-existing identities comes out in which situation—for instance—is my religious identity taking the front seat during this interaction, or is it my gender? Whether it is a subconscious choice or a decision made in the moment to highlight certain parts of the age-old question, "Who am I (in the social world)?", we noticed unique permutations and combinations of Venn diagrams emerging across the studies in this anthology.

More often than not, researchers fall into the trap of approaching the field from this rigid "insider vs outsider" binary; hence, we wanted to problematise and rethink the power flow on the field (Headland et al. 1990, cited in Clark, 2000). Practising critical reflexivity, that is, constantly questioning our own biases, assumptions, and the potential impact of our research on the researched community, allowed us to produce a holistic rhetoric. While preparing the questionnaire, as well as across the research cycle, we prioritised critical (self-)reflexivity and were constantly cognisant of our positionality on the field (Brewer, 1994; Schrock, 2013). Even though many forms of social identifiers, like class and caste, between the "us and them" varied, the few commonalities, such as gender, dismantled the unilateral flow of power. The respondents also took the driver's seat, in that they had the power to give away information which they, as subjects, considered the most important about their lives—we, as researchers, could only interpret this limited scope. One such instance where the insider-outsider dynamism can be extrapolated was when a team of female researchers went on a data collection expedition,

> On a particularly hot summer day, two of us [women] ventured out in the precarious Bawana colony of Delhi, alongside a male driver, to meet the Mahel family for a scheduled interview. Walking down the lanes to reach their home, we were met with peculiar glances and curious stares. Eventually, we located their home and were welcomed in graciously by Mrs. Mahel. While the vibrant hue of blue on the walls made the narrow living space warm and welcoming, we were greeted with a sense of dismissal and nonchalance. Mr. Mahel promptly sat on the bright red charpai and pointed us [ethnographers and the driver] towards the chairs that were put out. Meanwhile, Mrs. Mahel stood at the corner of the room, almost like a

> fly on the wall. Once everyone had assumed their place, we swiftly initiated an informal conversation with them.
>
> From the moment the interview began, Mr. Mahel would only look in the driver's direction while answering the questions. While we tried our best not to take it personally, it was almost as though he could not see us. As frustrating as it was, we knew we had to keep going. As the interview progressed, we realised that our expectations to converse with both of them were teased out of the park. To circumvent the seemingly inevitable alienation of Mrs. Mahel's voice from the narrative, we specifically directed a question towards her to hear her views as well. Unfortunately, though, we were met with a rhetorical question, "mujhe laga aap mujhse baat karne aaye ho." (I thought you had come here to interview me). Having heard praises about his unconventional and forward-looking attitude, which led the family to enrol their daughter on a vocational computer course, this lack of feminine autonomy in the household took us by surprise.

Being outsiders, the wariness Mr. Mahel displayed towards the researchers as individuals seemed only natural. However, as the interview unfolded, it gradually dawned on them that his apprehension was primarily directed at their identity as women. This encounter is by no means an isolated incident. In fact, forgoing the gender-specific challenges, most ethnographers in this anthology document such instances of unfamiliarity and passive hostility. These experiences are an integral part of the fieldwork process, compelling us to adapt swiftly and think on our feet.[1] While this is true for most field sites, it is especially pertinent to informal spaces.

In ethnographic research within informal spaces, hostility may manifest due to various factors. When the field ethnographers across studies extended this question to the community, the most common response was that their actions were led by the fear of exposure and exploitation. The power asymmetries (both socio-political and cultural in nature) in these spaces caused these groups to lie low and try to get by with what they were able to make in a day. Living from paycheck to paycheck, time has not necessarily been in their favour, limiting the prospects of what they can dream about. There was a general sense of hopelessness regarding any upward mobility financially, and, in most cases, aspirations were limited to educating one's children to break the cycle of destitution. We also

[1] It is to be noted that most ethnographers whose experience this book documents are women and that the experiences documented will thus be from their perspective.

observed that not having the resources to be aware of laws and regulations had made them wary of any and all people who appear "official", which most described as those who "*wear shirt and pants and ask a lot of questions*".

Through the course of the different ethnographies in this anthology, we were wary of the perils of simplifying complex narratives into one-dimensional representations of communities, cultures, and lifestyles. To do justice to the multifaceted experiences in informal spaces, and evade misunderstanding, prejudice, and misrepresentation, we actively tried to avoid the trap of a singular narrative. There are differences that fall through the cracks of the euro-centric development gaze which minismes the life of the "other" to a uniform encounter. As put forward by Nash (2011) and Lorde (1984), there are deeper issues situated at the heart of long-standing stories of oppression. History of such struggles was dictated by people with positions of power and those whose perspectives and experiences were documented, thus making it incomplete. Not including differences (of people and of geographies) in narrative dissemination will fuel further exclusion.

Hence, it was of utmost importance for us to avoid viewing the field solely with a lens of lack, that is, minimising the experiences of vulnerable communities to their protracted histories of adversity, denial of equitable access to resources, and a dearth of choices. To avoid driving ourselves into that corner, we steered clear of a preset research question before the initial visit. Rather, we entered the field with the skeletal questionnaire and built a final, tailored version after a preliminary survey and some unrecorded, informal conversations with the residents of the place. In fact, the first few visits were not necessarily about collecting data—instead, we tried to build connections with the community and familiarise ourselves with the power geometries[2] of the space. The preliminary findings were then compared to what has already been written about the community and their ecosystem, and a detailed questionnaire was developed with this feedback.

[2] Doreen Massey, a feminist geographer, conceptualised "power geometries" as the nuanced interplay of influence and authority within societies, shedding light on the intricate dynamics that exist between individuals and institutions. These subtle yet complex power relations have a profound impact on the lives of individuals and communities. The concept of power geometries serves as a pivotal framework for comprehending how spatiality and mobility are both shaped by and reproduce power differentials in society, facilitating the flow of privilege.

In an attempt to escape the trap of a singular narrative and not using the lens of lack, we tried to navigate this unpredictability of the field with the motto: the need *needs* to arise from the field. While the characteristics of the research team mentioned in this chapter (demographically varied and polyvocal) are important, we realised the community is still the "native informant" (Ghosh, 2016). What is lacking for us might not be a point of concern for those researched upon. In fact, we encountered instances where our expectations of the degree of distress were inflated compared to the communities' self-perception of the same. In the context of the Assam flood case study analysing the lives and livelihoods of *safai karamcharis* (sanitation workers), the research team initially anticipated a profoundly tumultuous condition in the community. Nevertheless, upon closer examination, a discerning observation emerged: the flooding disproportionately impacted only individuals residing in low-lying areas. For the broader sanitation community, this event did not evoke an extraordinary response; it was rather regarded as a routine occurrence. Notably, the community accorded lesser significance to the matter in comparison with the researchers' perspective.

In other cases, the respondents directed us to their struggles, which wasn't in our initial scope or a part of our secondary research. To get to this information, we had to make the respondents comfortable enough to delve into tangents about their labour and domestic concerns. In several case studies, a divergence between popular notions of the community and what they believe their hardships to be was noticed. Ghosh (2016) elaborates on feminist ethnographers promoting the idea of the Global South being capable of self-knowledge as a response to the inaccuracies of Western representation; a sentiment that can be equally extended to any two communities engaged in the study of one another. Additionally, Banerjee and Duflo (2012) wrote about the multitude of active choices households make despite being economically poor, which has been extrapolated into various fields to understand that the respondents are far from passive in the face of their circumstances. Overall, by taking into stride all the possible asymmetries between our position as academics and the respondent's position as those who willingly divulge information, we hoped to form a compelling nexus.

3 Conclusion

Overall, this section of the book analysed the utilisation of feminist ethnographic methods for conducting field studies in informal spaces in India during the pandemic. It delves into the thought process behind constructing a study, going off the paper and entering the field, and the trials and tribulations of materialising ideas along with the respondent community. Although various methodological concepts were used as part of the actual process of inquiry, in several cases, ethnographers reported needing to go off of their intuitions on the field for several key interactions, which later shaped how the case studies were conceptualised. Alongside the explicit data that we were able to gather in that duration, we got just as much implicit data; i.e. the behavioural cues which helped us decipher the social structures and power hierarchies that underscored the family unit.

Adhering to the course of action during our field study described in this chapter, we discerned the merits of presenting research findings through a plurality of narratives. Each individual case study in the manuscript, despite recording diverse anecdotes, is arranged in a coherent pattern to include a good harmony of ethnographer and informant experience. We have aspired to construct a narrative that involves each participant in the process to comprehend the alterations throughout the fieldwork process, and to document our findings in a sensitive manner, as opposed to relying solely on empirical data. The documentation and learnings from our ethnographies, we hope, will aggregate over time, and when read alongside complementary studies from the region, civil servants and policymakers could use those networks of knowledge to create an impact at the grassroots level.

References

Ahmed, S. (2006). *Queer Phenomenology: Orientations, Objects*. Duke University Press.

Arksey, H., & Knight, P. (1999). Interviewing for Social Scientists. *SAGE*. https://doi.org/10.4135/9781849209335

Avishai, O., Gerber, L., & Randles, J. (2013). The Feminist Ethnographer's Dilemma: Reconciling Progressive Research Agendas with Fieldwork Realities. *Journal of Contemporary Ethnography, 42*(4), 394–426. https://doi.org/10.1177/0891241612458955

Banerjee, A., & Duflo, E. (2012). *Poor Economics: A Radical Rethinking of the Way to Fight Global Poverty* (Reprint edition). PublicAffairs.

Basu, S. (2020, May 7). In Photos: As Lockdown Distress Continues, More Migrants Begin Walking Home. *The Wire*. https://thewire.in/rights/migrants-walking-photos-lockdown-covid-19

Benson, K., & Nagar, R. (2006). Collaboration as Resistance? Reconsidering the Processes, Products, and Possibilities of Feminist Oral History and Ethnography. *Gender, Place & Culture, 13*(5), 581–592. https://doi.org/10.1080/09663690600859083

Brewer, J. D. (1994). The Ethnographic Critique of Ethnography: Sectarianism in the Ruc. *Sociology, 28*(1), 231–244.

Clark, J. (2000). *Beyond Empathy: An Ethnographic Approach to Cross-Cultural Social Work Practice* [Unpblished Manuscript]. https://citeseerx.ist.psu.edu/document?repid=rep1&type=pdf&doi=66c62701aa08e616183de9516fdf39920f99a2cb

Crawley, S. L. (2012). Autoethnography as Feminist Self-Interview. In J. F. Gubrium, J. A. Holstein, A. B. Marvasti, & K. D. McKinney (Eds.), *The SAGE Handbook of Interview Research: The Complexity of the Craft*. SAGE. https://doi.org/10.4135/9781452218403

Davis, D.-A., & Craven, C. (2016). *Feminist Ethnography: Thinking Through Methodologies, Challenges, and Possibilities*. Rowman & Littlefield.

Denzin, N. K. (2014). *Interpretive Autoethnography* (2nd ed.). SAGE. https://doi.org/10.4135/9781506374697

Fetterman, D. M. (2010). *Ethnography: Step-by-Step* (3rd ed., Vol. 17). Sage.

Geertz, C. (1973). *The Interpretation of Cultures*. Basic Books.

Ghosh, S. T. (2016). Feminist Ethnography. In *The Wiley Blackwell Encyclopedia of Gender and Sexuality Studies* (pp. 1–9). John Wiley & Sons. https://doi.org/10.1002/9781118663219.wbegss765

Günel, G., Varma, S., & Watanabe, C. (2020, June 9). A Manifesto for Patchwork Ethnography. *Society for Cultural Anthropology, Member Voices, Fieldsights*. https://culanth.org/fieldsights/a-manifesto-for-patchwork-ethnography

Hamal, S. (2020). Trust in Ethnography: Narrating the Difficulties, Rewards and Dilemmas of Entry, Engagement and Exit (3Es) in the Research Field. *Dhaulagiri Journal of Sociology and Anthropology, 14*, 97–105. https://doi.org/10.3126/dsaj.v14i0.28521

Harding, S. (1987). Introduction: Is There a Feminist Methodology? In S. Harding (Ed.), *Feminism and Methodology* (pp. 1–14). Indiana University Press.

Headland, T. N., Pike, K. L., & Harris, M. (Eds.). (1990). *Emics and Etics: The Insider/Outsider Debate* (p. 226). Sage.

Heath, M., Darkwah, A., Beoku-Betts, J., & Purkayastha, B. (Eds.). (2022). *Global Feminist Autoethnographies During COVID-19: Displacements and Disruptions*. Routledge. https://www.routledge.com/Global-Feminist-Autoethnographies-During-COVID-19-Displacements-and-Disruptions/Heath-Darkwah-Beoku-Betts-Purkayastha/p/book/9781032122656

Hosokawa, F. (2010). *Building Trust: Doing Research to Understand Ethnic Communities*. Lexington Books.

Lems, A. (2020, June 11). *The (Im)possibility of Ethnographic Research during Corona*. Max Planck Institute for Social Anthropology. https://www.eth.mpg.de/5478478/news-2020-06-11-01

Lorde, A. (1984). *Sister Outsider*. Crossing Press.

Lutzoni, L. (2016). In-formalised Urban Space Design. Rethinking the Relationship between Formal and Informal. *City, Territory and Architecture, 3*(1), 20. https://doi.org/10.1186/s40410-016-0046-9

Nash, J. C. (2011). Practicing Love: Black Feminism, Love-Politics, and Post-Intersectionality. *Meridians, 11*(2), 1–24. https://doi.org/10.2979/meridians.11.2.1

Rodrik, D. (2023). *On Productivism* (HKS Working Paper No. RWP23-012). Harvard University, Harvard Kennedy School (HKS). https://doi.org/10.2139/ssrn.4404241

Schrock, R. D. (2013). The Methodological Imperatives of Feminist Ethnography. *Journal of Feminist Scholarship, 5*(Fall), 54–60.

Shaw, P., & Hudson, J. (2009, July 4). *The Qualities of Informal Space: (Re)appropriation within the Informal, Interstitial Spaces of the City*. Occupation: Negotiations with Constructed Space, University of Brighton.

Siddiqui, D. (2020, April 22). In Pictures: The Long Road Home for India's Migrant Workers. *Al Jazeera*. https://www.aljazeera.com/gallery/2020/4/22/in-pictures-the-long-road-home-for-indias-migrant-workers

Spivak, G. C. (1985). The Rani of Sirmur: An Essay in Reading the Archives. *History and Theory, 24*(3), 247–272. https://doi.org/10.2307/2505169

Spradley, J. P., & McCurdy, D. W. (Eds.). (2012). *Culture and Ethnography* (14th ed.). Jill Potash.

Sumesh, S. S., & Gogoi, N. (2022). Collecting the 'Thick Descriptions': A Pandemic Ethnography of the Lived Experiences of Covid-19 Induced Stigma and Social Discrimination in India. *Journal of Loss and Trauma, 27*(3), 271–284. https://doi.org/10.1080/15325024.2021.1947019

The Long Walk of India's Migrant Workers in Covid-Hit 2020. (2020, December 25). *The Indian Express*. https://indianexpress.com/article/india/the-long-walk-of-indias-migrant-workers-in-covid-hit-2020-7118809/

CHAPTER 3

Navigating Through Shocks: *Mīṉavar* of Tamil Nadu and Pondicherry

Sakshi Chindaliya, Ashika Thomas, Deepanshu Mohan, and Jignesh Mistry

Abstract This study is a culmination of an ethnographic research that was conducted on fisherfolk in parts of Tamil Nadu and Puducherry during the two-month annual ban-period (April–June). It captures the nuances of lives and livelihoods of this community as they juggle a hectic work

S. Chindaliya (✉) · D. Mohan
Jindal School of Liberal Arts and Humanities, O.P. Jindal Global University, Sonipat, India
e-mail: sakshichindaliya@yahoo.in

D. Mohan
e-mail: dmohan@jgu.edu.in

D. Mohan · J. Mistry
Centre for New Economics Studies, Jindal School of Liberal Arts And Humanities, Jindal Global University, Sonipat, India
e-mail: jignesh1104@gmail.com

A. Thomas
London School of Economics and Political Science, London, UK
e-mail: ashikathms@gmail.com

D. Mohan et al. (eds.), *Pan-India Stories of Informal Workers During Covid-19 Pandemic*, https://doi.org/10.1007/978-981-97-1525-1_3

schedule with constant and recurring shocks. Exploring the intricacies of socio-economic and cultural portfolios on fishers in this region has helped in documenting the issues and challenges that confront them. This has also aided in dismantling some preconceived notions about the community and bringing forward fishers' diverse personal narratives. Money management, gender polarities and youth participation and its effects on the continuity of trade is analyzed. Additionally, the paper delves into assessing the dynamics of the changing climate conditions and rampant marine pollution on fishers and the trade at large. Finally, the research juxtaposes the 2004 Tsunami with the 2020 Covid Pandemic to assess temporal vulnerabilities and discusses the requirement for ex-post and preventive policy measures to deal with shocks.

Keywords Fishing · Tamil Nadu and Puducherry · Gender polarity · Climate crisis · Marine pollution · Covid-19 pandemic · Feminist ethnography

1 Introduction

In the peak of the summer of 2021, most tourists and travellers (abiding by pandemic restrictions) sought respite at some of the pristine beaches of Tamil Nadu and Puducherry. Siddharth, who loved eating fish growing up, went away to Pondicherry for a vacation and felt that he had a rare opportunity to visit and interact with a community he did not have access to in Gurgaon (his current city of residence). Through his excursions he began observing the peculiar gender dynamics and the treacherous nature of the fishing industry prominent in the area. In interacting with the fishers, he discovered stories that were often invisibilised from the mainstream discourse. Thus began the journey of two ethnographers—Siddharth and Jignesh—navigating through the overlooked shores to gauge the life and lifestyle of fisherfolk. Spending over two months in the state, they took the same routes to reach the same destinations and asked similar questions. Somewhere amidst the repetitive mundanity of their actions, not only were they able to immerse themselves into the customs and culture of the place, but also learn about what it means to be a fisher in that region.

In India, the fishing sector provides employment to around 28 million people, including inland and marine fishers (Handbook on Fisheries Statistics, 2020). It is the second largest producer of fish in the world, contributing 7.58% to the global market and 7.28% to the domestic agricultural Gross Value Added (GVA) (Economic Survey 2020–2021). Despite appearing as a thriving industry, most fisherfolk at the frontlines, carrying the burdens of the job, are forced to succumb to sub-par conditions. While they facilitate its production and market, they are confronted by issues including but not limited to, unpredictable environmental hazards, insufficient financial capital, and a dearth of infrastructural resources (Noman et al., 2020).

As is any other demographic in India, it is imperative to recognise that workers in the fishing communities are not a homogenous group. The prevailing socio-cultural hierarchies in the sector, such as caste-class-gender identities, make some more vulnerable than others (Cánovas-Molina & García-Frapolli, 2022; Islam et al., 2013; Umaheshwari et al., 2021; Zacharia et al., 2016). Small-Scale Fishers (SSF) have been documented to be more susceptible to the unfavourable circumstances mentioned above (Image 1). About 95% of the fishing industry in developing countries comprises of SSF, making them the focus of this study. An SSF is characterised by self-owned rudimentary fishing gear, minimal capital investment, reliance on indigenous knowledge, dependence on interconnected local markets and dismal socio-economic factors (Matthew, 2015).

Within India, Tamil Nadu and Puducherry are home to approximately 803,033 and 76,772 fishers, respectively (Handbook on Fisheries Statistics, 2020). In the two-month period we had spent covering the coasts of Tamil Nadu and parts of Pondicherry, we came across many fishing communities with their own stories to tell about everything ranging from past shocks to new ones, current politics to changing environment conditions, all of which affect their lives to a great extent. The findings gave insights into their economic choices, gender-polar trends in the sector and the youth's perception of the trade. The study also explored the abysmal conditions of coastal space due to marine pollution and the climate crisis. Finally, the chapter inspected the repercussions of the 2004 tsunami and the COVID-19 pandemic and the response, highlighting the long-lasting adverse effects and the consequent slow recovery.

Image 1 Fishers sailing out for a day at the sea (Photograph by Jignesh Mistry)

2 Location

We explored the fishing hamlets of Thandiraayan Kuppam, Chinna Mudaliyar Chavadi, and Killai in Tamil Nadu and Vaithikuppam and Kurichikuppam, in Puducherry, respectively. On the first day, the team visited the villages of Vaithikuppam and Kurichikuppam, located immediately to the north of Rock Beach and Promenade Beach in Puducherry, which are popular tourist destinations. The beaches were marked by an abundance of tourists and were home to various restaurants, hotels and shops, along with other local attractions. These two villages come under the Raj Bhavan constituency of the Puducherry Assembly, the residence of the Governor. These areas were also situated adjacent to the sewage outlets for the state of Puducherry, and the disposal site for the cargo vessels that dock at the harbour. Being major hubs for small-scale fishing in Puducherry, they host the Tsunami Quarters built by the Government where most of the fishing families live. The community housing was built after the tsunami that struck these spaces on December 26, 2004.

Puducherry has four predominant fish markets—the primary Goubert Fish Market, the secondary H. M. Kassim, Ambour Salai (formerly known as the Senji Salai) and Lawspet Fish markets. The main market is solely reserved for approximately 360 women fish sellers from Vaithikuppam, Kurichikuppam and Vambakeerapalayam. The trade centres serve as the place where fish sellers come early in the morning to collect their yield by participating in auctions or wholesale trade. The markets were sectioned into three distinct spaces—one to sell fresh fish, the other to sell dry and brined ones, (locally called *Karuvaadu*), and another to clean the yield. The roles taken up by the fish sellers were strict; a cleaner could not sell, and vice-versa (Image 2).

Next, the ethnographers went along the coast of Serenity Beach and Quiet Beach, visiting the Thandirayan Kuppam and Chinna Mudaliyar Chavadi villages, respectively, situated in the Viluppuram district of Tamil Nadu. Post-2004, fishers in this area began residing at the Tsunami quarters. The fisherfolk of Thandirayan Kuppam chose to sell the fish along the Serenity Beach itself, right after the men docked the boat. Whereas, in Chinna Mudaliyar Chavadi, fishers prefer to sell their catch through auctions, where the primary participants are women. The auctions take

Image 2 A customer waits for a woman who sells fish at the Goubert Fish Market (Photograph by Jignesh Mistry)

place at the podium built by the community, which is situated close to the temple dedicated to the village guardian deity.

When Jignesh and Siddharth visited these sites, the bidding began at 6 A.M. sharp, and the highest bid was paid to the fishermen on the same day. The sellers returned the next day with the sale price and their profits. The site was managed by a village committee member who also handled the transactions during the auction. They were also responsible for collecting 10% of the auction money as part of a community fund to develop common spaces and fund the village festivals. The annual selection of the member also happened through a rigorous auction process, where the highest bidder for the position gets it. In turn, the remainder share of the community fund went into his pocket as reimbursement (Image 3).

The village of Killai, which the ethnographers ultimately visited, is situated in the Cuddalore district of Tamil Nadu, along the Uppanaru River and across the Pichavaram Mangrove Forests. Fishermen here are involved in both riverside and marine fishing. While the village has predominantly

Image 3 A fisherwoman bidding at the auction site on the shores of Serenity Beach (Photograph by Jignesh Mistry)

fishermen belonging to the Most Backward Caste (MBC), the particular focus lies on the Irulas, an Adivasi group who were originally hunter-gatherers. This community migrated from the forests of Andhra Pradesh as labourers who worked in the coconut and palm plantations. As the Government banned the hunting of snakes in the 1970s, this community adopted fishing as their occupation with the help of the Forest Department (The Wild Life Protection Act, 1972). The Irulas, who occupy two of the twelve blocks of the village, are considered responsible for the expansion of the Mangrove Forests. This eventually led to the village being saved from the massive destruction inflicted by the tsunami (United Nations Team for Tsunami Recovery Support, 2006).

3 Methodology

Siddharth and Jignesh visited Thandiraayan Kuppam, Chinna Mudaliyar Chavadi, Killai, Vaithikuppam and Kurichikuppam at the height of the second wave of the COVID-19 pandemic and the start of the annual 61-day ban period, between 15 April and 15 June. A fishing ban is imposed in this area for these two months, as the fish in this region often copulate during this period or are in juvenile stages. Only Small-Scale Fishers (SSFs) with sanctioned fibre boats were allowed to venture into the sea during specific hours in the ban period. Due to limited working opportunities, fisherfolk had more spare time. Siddharth realised that this period was ideal for having in-depth conversations with willing participants. Thus, with the hope to unpack the gendered-trends and youth aspirations, we dipped into the precarity of these vulnerable spaces.

> He commented, "While it started as a project out of personal interest alone, I knew that two heads are better than one. After Ashika and Sakshi joined the team, the intuitive idea fleshed out in a theoretical sense. Sakshi had knowledge of the anthropocene, pollution, and sustainability and Ashika brought up patterns in income and consumption based on Banerjee and Duflo's past works. These are things that I hadn't previously considered. I started feeling certain that our backgrounds in different disciplines would merge at a crossroad, making the narrative more holistic- you could blame it on our liberal arts training, I suppose."

Approaching the field from a feminist ethnographic perspective, detailed observations were recorded in conjunction with around 30 semi-structured interviews. These were conducted based on a comprehensive questionnaire, allowing for more in-depth research that let the participants explore their awareness of their positions and avoid the misrecognition of the information provided. This methodology helped to combat the ethical conundrum of a power imbalance between the researcher and the participants, as is often the case. Ensuring the co-production of knowledge gave the respondents a sense of agency over their experiences, allowing for two-way dissemination of information (Arksey & Knight, 1999).

The questionnaire was designed after collating trends and patterns from a few preliminary visits. The parameters of the study follow the Coulthard et al. framework on well-being. As suggested, we focused on observing communities' overall wellness as opposed to just economic aspects, giving a more 'holistic and person-centred analysis' (Coulthard et al., 2018: 246). Simultaneously, we also explored previous research on the local fishing community, specifically the studies conducted by the French Institute of Pondicherry (IFP). During the fieldwork phase, Siddharth also reached out to IFP and got in touch with Dr. Senthil Babu, who connected us with his associates and field contacts, facilitating the building of our networks of knowledge.

We collected an equal sample of 15 fishermen, who engage in the fishing practice, and 15 fisherwomen, who run the sales and the market, to get balanced perspectives. The interactions revealed new and previously unexplored trends in polarities, uncertainties and the continuity of this trade. Jignesh commented on building varying connections to ensure polyvocality in the narrative,

> Siddharth and I together, we traversed the area, actively seeking out and conversing with the community members. Our objective was to introduce ourselves consistently, ensuring our presence was well-noted. In the course of our interactions, we spoke to several fisherfolk at the docks and market spaces. In tandem to that, we encountered a fishing union, and sought their insights on the pandemic restrictions within the region. Interestingly, towards the end of our discussion, we discovered that the person was affiliated with the DMK political party and held a leadership position within the union. Similarly, many interactions while finding points of contact involved individuals who had affiliations with political groups. This pattern seems to be prevalent in most areas we visited. Subsequently, we inquired about the possibility of speaking with other notable figures within the union, but only received minimal support. Nevertheless, our perseverance allowed us

to engage with other stakeholders. We had also simultaneously set out to explore various facets of the fishing community; including their residential colonies, boat docking areas, fish markets, and fish auction sites.

During the initial phases of our research cycle, the field ethnographers exercised considerable caution in tempering any preconceived notions harboured regarding the respondents. This deliberate effort was undertaken to avoid using leading questions for our inquiries, thereby preserving the authenticity of the narrative. This dynamic was especially complex in this context as one of the field ethnographers, Siddharth, was a part of the Tamil cultural milieu. Unlike cross-cultural studies, where one would imagine a comprehensive understanding of the socio-cultural dynamics of their own people, pursuing fieldwork in adjacent geographical spaces can also pose unique challenges. Siddharth, who used to live in the state, extrapolated on this complex positionality,

> I was born and brought up in Tamil Nadu for 16 years and I have seen a lot of Tamil movies. The preconceived notions regarding fishing villages in such popular media was that they were terrible people- who one should be wary of. They are depicted as rogues, rowdies and running illegal businesses and that it's dangerous to talk to them; while the union leaders would carry weapons and one wrong statement would lead them to hurt you. Films tend to have such ugly stereotypes. Growing up, I was always told that these communities will dismiss you and if you still persisted they get offended easily- they gang up against you. As much as I was smiling during the initial recce, I was scared. However, extended conversations soon broke these notions for me.

Since Siddharth was aware of his manufactured perceptions, he preemptively took precautions to avoid the trap of a singular narrative. The influence of Jignesh in the team, who had no previous engagement with the community but a distant understanding of the mainstream culture, helped in striking the much-needed balance of narratives. Jignesh was able to pick out behaviours and patterns which were normalised for Siddharth, and meanwhile, Siddharth helped in making sense of them. The synergy of the "insider-outsider" duo, alongside the backend team, helped in circumventing some pressing challenges.

> "I can look at and collect stories and collect answers to the questionnaire that we framed. However, at the end of the day it is a very tiring

process. I needed people who were looking at the interactions from an external perspective. Mentally, it was draining going out in the morning and coming back in the evening and thus having fresh perspectives on what was important was difficult. Knowing the language helped me translate the information unto Jignesh and the backend team who then processed it." explained Siddharth.

Despite managing to actively avoid falling into the traps of community stereotypes, interactions still proved to be cumbersome. Engaging in meaningful conversations posed a challenge, primarily due to the preference for the Tamil language among the locals. The team, therefore, had to navigate and understand the respondents while also being respectful of their space. Consequently, fisherfolk working in various established field sites had to be approached very differently, ranging from casual off-the-record conversations to more structured group interviews. Both Siddharth and Jignesh had varying experiences in this regard:

> "So as a person who is not from the region in enquiry, I was lucky to understand the language that was spoken there which really helped. The few things I obviously did was go around Pondicherry, especially Kadloor and other such districts. The people who worked there helped a lot. I asked the receptionist who was luckily enough originally from a fishing village himself who then gave me the numbers of a few future respondents.Through him I also took an initial look at the markets and fishing places. The way networks were built was having conversations with anyone at specific locations like the beach. I would deduce who were locals and who were tourists and observe and talk to them.", explained Siddharth.

Meanwhile, Jignesh's retrospective understanding of his experience was,

> While Siddharth has proficiency in Tamil, I actively sought conversations conducted in Hindi or English to facilitate better comprehension on my part. Regrettably, my knowledge of Tamil (or lack thereof) extended only to a complete lack of understanding. Even though I had the advantage of a team member who could comprehend Tamil, his familiarity with the nuances of the local dialects was limited. As an ethnographer, I found it challenging to rely extensively on a translator. My predicament lay in the necessity of peering into their eyes, attempting to connect with their emotions, and deciphering the unspoken messages they conveyed.

However, despite the challenges to establish rapport, the ethnographers made it a daily routine to visit the fish markets, not only to familiarise themselves with the surroundings but also to acquaint the respondents with their presence. Over time, they endeavoured to cultivate meaningful relationships with select respondents, hoping they would provide them with valuable information and provide access to their networks. Despite Siddharth's partial familiarity, both Jignesh and Siddharth sensed hesitancy and resistance from the community and thus, primarily aimed to build trust. Time, in this context, was on our side and became the biggest rescue through this journey. The on-field researchers set out to conduct visits during early mornings as the fishers were most available then. The ethnographers also conveyed our affiliation with an educational institution and a research centre, underscoring our genuine interest in starting a conversation with them.

> "I remember this one fisherman who was ready to help us but not at the get go. I took him around Pondicherry on my scooter so that he would help me interact with his network. Once that trust was built with one respondent, his circle of family and friends were willing to participate.", Siddharth recounted.
>
> Jignesh also added, "Younger fishermen were the most willing participants- metric to college graduates. They mistook us for youtubers, but when we had a questionnaire and explained who we were, they were quite helpful and took us to the tsunami quarters-the colony which was made for fisherfolk. We also met their senior family members at the boat docking area."

Before the trust-building exercise, when the ethnographers were truly "outsiders", they tried to get past the initial hesitancy by building on their observations and using that to leverage conversations with the community. They were actively searching for fishers who were willing to share stories and add to the ethnographer's existing knowledge. Jignesh recalls the preliminary impression of the field sites,

> Initially, the hesitation among the community members was very visible. We had a section in the questionnaire about monthly expenditures. Understanding that this may be a sensitive topic, we visited auction sites, and beaches on our own without a guide. We got an early idea about the catch and the sale mechanisms simply through observation. We also got a sense

> of fishers' everyday spending on loaders, unloaders, nets, diesel, ice, transport, etc. It gave us a pretty good idea about their finance structure as these were daily transactions which they incurred. Visiting the markets also helped us understand the kind of fish sold by women and the amount as well. While they were hesitant at first, once we proved that we were familiar with the system and up-to-date with the market dynamics, they slowly but surely began opening up.

While most of the data collection process went smoothly, we faced some challenges. There were instances of squabbles between the interviewee and persons in the surroundings who did not necessarily agree with their answers. To avoid this, most interviews were conducted in isolation. This approach was not only compliant to the pandemic restrictions but also helped garner the respondents' trust, assuring them that the information provided and observed would not be brought up against them at any point and was purely for research purposes.

> Conflicts weren't hands-on or explicit per se. Rather, we prudently sidestepped certain discussions upon detecting tense situations. Our overarching approach was to avoid confrontation whenever feasible. In instances where particular respondents raised questions about our presence and grew vocally assertive, we exercised discretion by withdrawing for the day, with the intention of resuming discussions with more amicable individuals at a later time. Occasionally, some fisherfolk would explicitly instruct us to depart from the premises, and we duly complied. Striking the delicate balance between listening to their concerns and discerning the appropriate moment to withdraw was an ongoing challenge. It is imperative to note that this does not entail outright abandonment of the conversation, as deciphering the underlying reasons for a respondent's resistance to our inquiries may hold intrinsic significance.
>
> A pertinent example arose during our visits to the fish market, where a woman assumed the role of the union leader. She observed our daily presence with an air of suspicion, even after we had clarified the nature of our research. Furthermore, she lodged complaints about our activities with fellow fisherwomen, warning them against engaging with us. Despite initially indicating her willingness to engage in dialogue, she renounced her promise, asserting, "You are not meant to be here," and registering her disapproval of our daily presence as a disturbance to the established atmosphere." Such occurrences, as Jignesh aptly noted, while anticipated, always managed to pose unique challenges.

Despite the occasional obstacles and resistance we encountered, cultural sensitivity guided our mobility across this time and space. It allowed us to navigate the unpredictable field and showcase a multidimensional portrayal of a community that is often misunderstood or oversimplified.

4 Observations, Findings and Analysis

The feminist ethnographic research conducted holds a mirror to the general trends and priorities of fisherfolk. This section will unravel the economic, social and environmental circumstances of such communities loosely based on the dimensions of well-being as posited by Coulthard et al. (2018). Acknowledging that the fisherfolk have agency over their own choices and exercise this to achieve their desired standard of living within their capabilities, this study looks at the following trends.

4.1 Lifestyle

A typical day in a fisher's life begins at around 3:00 A.M. Before the crack of dawn, fishermen venture into the sea and do not return to the shore until between 8 and 10 A.M. Post-catching the fresh yield, they auction the catch, visit the fish markets, detangle nets and prepare their gear for the following day. Often over 12 hours, the cumbersome workday leaves them with something to be desired. During the day, fishers attempt to find time to unwind, rest, manage sleep and fulfil their dietary requirements. At night, most fisherfolk retire to bed at around 10:00 P.M., nervously anticipating the day to follow. Almost all fishers who were interviewed commented that they manage to sleep for approximately 6 hours per day. It is important to note that these 6 hours include their afternoon sleep time and are often interrupted. This leads to various short- and long-term physical and mental health consequences (Medic et al., 2017).

As much as their work is time-based, fisherfolk do not have the luxury of planning their day or ending it at the desired time. 'The day-to-day variability in activities due to uncontrollable factors, such as fishing success, repairing gear and weather conditions, means that pre-planned duty schedules are often not respected' (Gander et al., 2009: 397). One can always find fisherfolk struggling with things such as variability in the amount of fish caught, detangling plastic from nets and gauging the tides, among other things. These factors are entirely out of their control, and uncertainties in their conditions are reflected in their unbalanced dietary trends. Nutritional requirements in these parts are primarily drawn from rice, fermented rice-based dishes and pulses like *Toor Dal* (pigeon pea). Fish is the most frequently consumed animal protein in these communities. Minimal vegetable and fruit intake could be a sign of vitamin and fibre deficiency, which is also found to be the case in fishing communities in other parts of India (Patro et al., 2020).

4.2 *Budgeting*[1]

Despite their variable daily income, the fisherfolk actively make choices on how to delegate the money to their fixed commitments and other spending. Borrowing from Banerjee and Duflo's *Poor Economics* line of thought, there is a need to look at what the fisherfolk wish to do, their everyday choices, and trade-offs and engage in policy-making accordingly. Despite having meagre incomes and surviving on rice gruel for a significant part of the year, these communities, with around four members per household on average, still choose to make sizable alternate expenses. They borrow money to engage in festivals, community activities and hold weddings, compromising what would otherwise be considered essential spending (food, clothing, etc.) (Banerjee & Duflo, 2011). In fact, one of the respondents commented, 'I cannot determine how much I spend on socio-cultural activities. Essentially, I look at how much my relatives are spending and spend a little more than that'.[2] Even at low levels of income, agency is exercised, and the social dynamics play an imperative role in the choices made.

Essential Spending: Water, Food, Electricity and Clothing: This category covers spending required for sustenance that every household will incur at least to a certain degree. Rent/spending on residence is left out because the respondents either live in their own homes or the Tsunami Quarters set up by the state government. Based on the responses, on average, a family in the fishing community spends Rs. 14,821, Rs. 399, Rs. 847 and Rs. 1127 on food, water, electricity and clothing, respectively. The graph shows the individual essential spending of each household. It

[1] This section considers household expenditure as a whole since income is often pooled and individual expenses are very rare.

[2] This quotation and all quotations henceforth have been translated from Tamil.

is interesting to note that there is a visible variation in living standards among a community otherwise considered to be a homogenous group (even when accounting for the number of household members) (Fig. 1)

Evidently, the expenditure on food is significantly higher (86.2%) than other essential requirements of water (2.3%), electricity (4.9%) and clothing (6.6%). One of the main reasons behind this disproportionate expenditure is the inadequate Public Distribution Systems (ration shops)[3] available in the area. Respondents reported that the quality of food available at these government facilities is abysmal. They only frequent the establishment to avail portions of sub-par quality rice, which they later resell to the local rice batter manufacturers for a minimal price.

Education: A massive portion of fisherfolk's expenditure can be attributed to education-related spending. While fishers themselves did not get the opportunity to access formal education systems, they are persistent

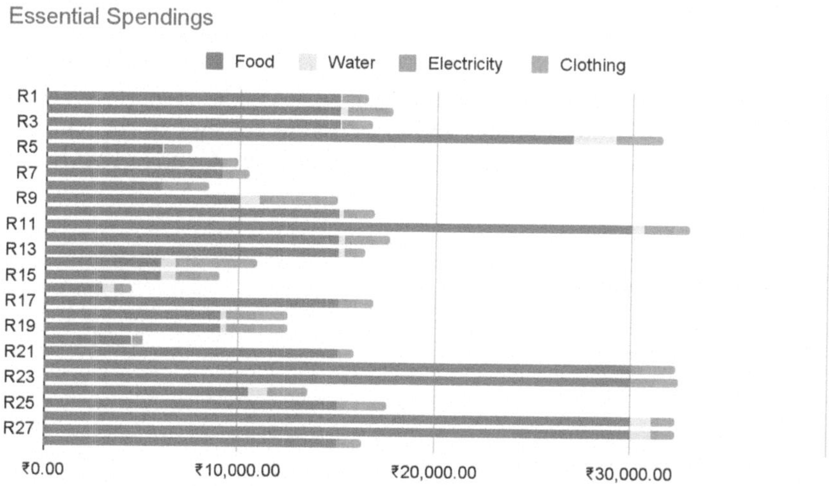

Fig. 1 Month-wise spending of 30 respondents on food, water, electricity and clothing

[3] Public Distribution System (PDS) is a food distribution channel set up by the Government of India initially in the 1960s and expanded later in the 1970s and 1980s. Its aim is to minimise food insecurity by providing it at subsidised prices. Specifically for the state of Tamil Nadu and Puducherry respondents report that the government has issued red cards for individuals earning less than Rs. 15,000 per annum and yellow cards otherwise.

that their children hone varied skills to prepare for a wider job market. Contrary to Banerjee and Duflo's argument, fisherfolk actively invest in education at all levels and expect high returns (Banerjee & Duflo, 2011). This could be attributed to the uncertainties of the fishing profession and the lack of security in income. Figure 2 shows the spending on education per household. The variability of the graph is due to the difference in the number of children per household and their respective enrolment levels. A few respondents were not making active investments in the education of any of their kin, but they have done so in the past. As seen, fisherfolk are spending exponentially more on their children's education to escape this generational cycle of uncertainty. Nuances in the comparative education patterns across generations will be explored in the section covering youth participation.

Health: The average monthly household health expenditure amounts to Rs. 3518, and Fig. 3 depicts the household-wise breakdown. This covers any expenditure incurred for treating injuries that occur during their time in the sea and treatment of chronic occupational illnesses prevalent in these households. Some respondents also commented on having to take loans for any unprecedented emergency surgeries. Fisherfolk access government and private hospitals and dispensaries to cater to their health and well-being needs. The closest Primary Healthcare Centre (PHC) was

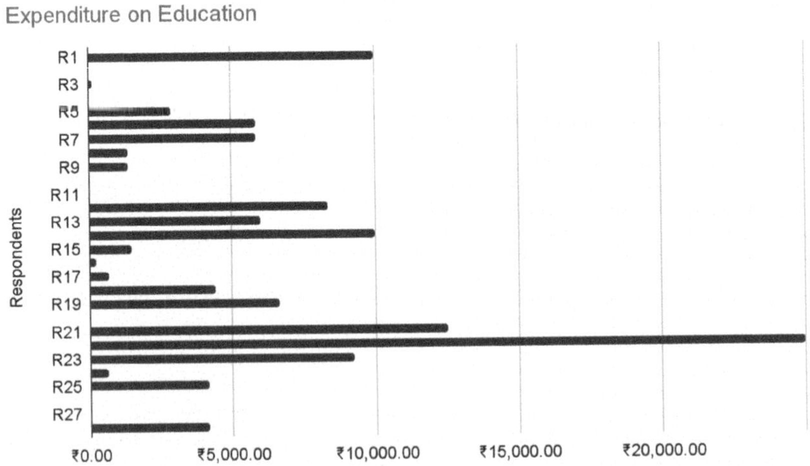

Fig. 2 Month-wise spending of 30 respondents on their children's education

reported to be in their vicinity, approximately 1.5 km from the housing quarters. While the target communities for primary health centres in the rest of the country consider the institution to be defunct, those on the coast of Puducherry and Tamil Nadu seem to be largely meeting their required needs at subsidised rates. When asked about their preference, 72% of the fisherfolk reported frequenting the government-run PHCs, while the remaining 28% prefer private institutions.

Business Related: Transportation and Reinvestment into Business: Continuation of any trade is dependent on paying for the means that facilitate it and the subsequent reinvestments made. Figure 4 showcases a monthly breakdown of expenditure on transport and other industry-related payments made. Transportation is required by all on a daily basis to carry yield from the auction sites to the marketplaces and export centres. On the other hand, reinvestment includes repairing any damages to boats, replenishing fuel stocks, maintaining fishing nets and restocking resources using tools such as ice boxes. A small set of fisherfolk have not upgraded their gear in years and are forced to work with the wear and tear. Many of these resources, especially boats, are rented owing to the fisherfolk's inability to pay large sums at once.

Loans: Considering the unpredictable nature of their work and income, fishers are pushed to take credit from both formal and informal entities

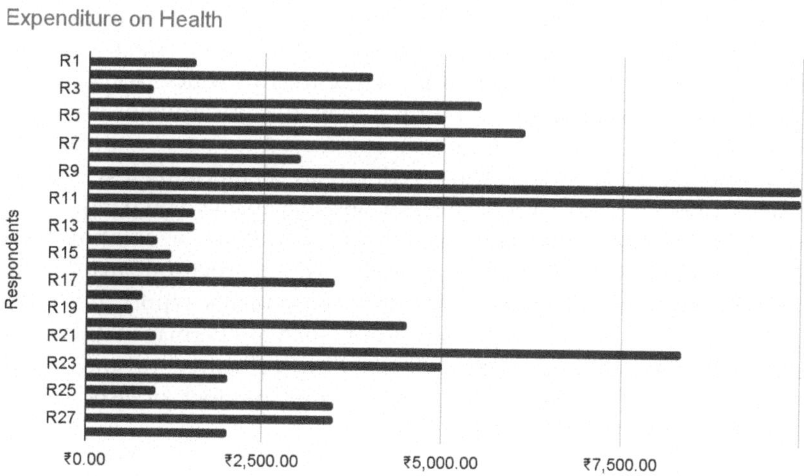

Fig. 3 Month-wise spending of 30 respondents on health-related activities

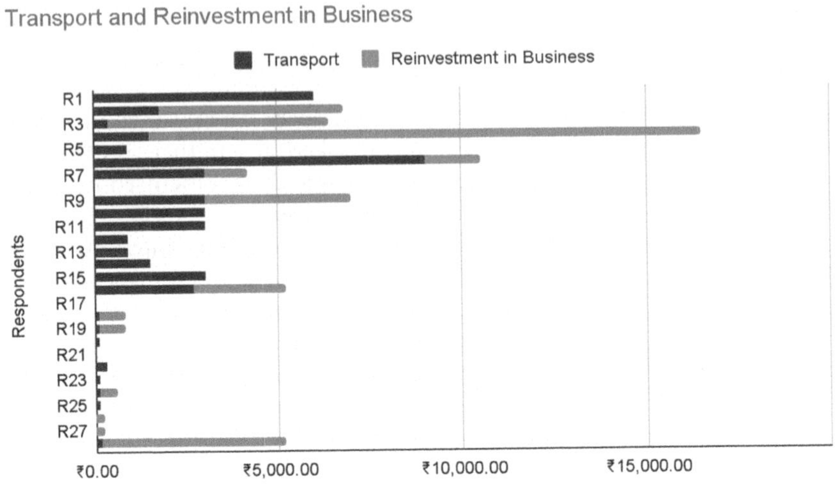

Fig. 4 Month-wise expenditure on business-related matters

to make ends meet. This could be due to various factors, as shown in Fig. 5. Firstly, sizable loans are taken on business-related matters with the expectation of receiving good returns. Unsurprisingly, however, it is to no avail. Secondly, there is a constant dependence on loans to meet essential household demands (12.5% from Fig. 5). This is a sign of an eventual debt trap[4] due to the recurring expenditures, which leave no room for dependence on credits for emergencies or other facets of life. Finally, as most respondents currently live in the government-provided Tsunami Quarters, fisherfolk have not considered moving to a privately owned property. Home loans, thus credited, are significantly less (8.3%).

Fishers borrow from various institutions, like banks (66.67%), small financial institutions (20%) and pawn brokers (6.67%) or combinations of these (6.66%). Most find it moderately easy to procure loans despite the evident lack of collateral—only three respondents report any difficulty. Usually, houses and citizenship proofs such as (Permanent Account Number [PAN], Aadhaar or Ration card) are presented to and documented by these financial institutions. A large number of fishers, not

[4] Debt Trap here refers to the situation of having to take fresh loans to pay off existing ones.

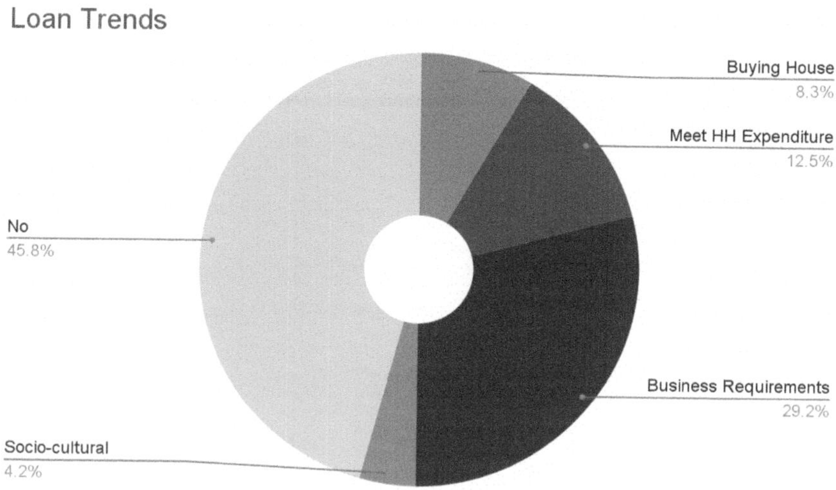

Fig. 5 Loan trends among the fishing community in Tamil Nadu and Puducherry(*Note* 'HH' here refers to 'household')

represented by these numbers, borrow money informally from their relatives and friends to tide over.

Cultural and Leisure: Amidst their hectic days and sleepless nights, fishers seek out opportunities they can resort to for some relief. Since fishing work is unpredictable, they spend a significant amount on activities which can be integrated into their daily routine. This primarily includes buying liquor and frequenting cinema houses for men, and women occasionally partake in local, women-only board games. In addition to that, fisherfolk do not inhibit themselves from making payments for socio-cultural activities. Considering that they wish to maintain their status quo in society, they even go as far as taking loans for weddings and festival celebrations. Figure 6 depicts these trends for the 30 respondents interviewed.

Total Monthly Spending: To wrap up, the average monthly expenditure for fisher households across all these indicators comes down to Rs. 32,175 per month. Considering the inflation in the country and variability in their income, they are posed with several challenges. The ban-period relief fund provided by the state government adds up to Rs.

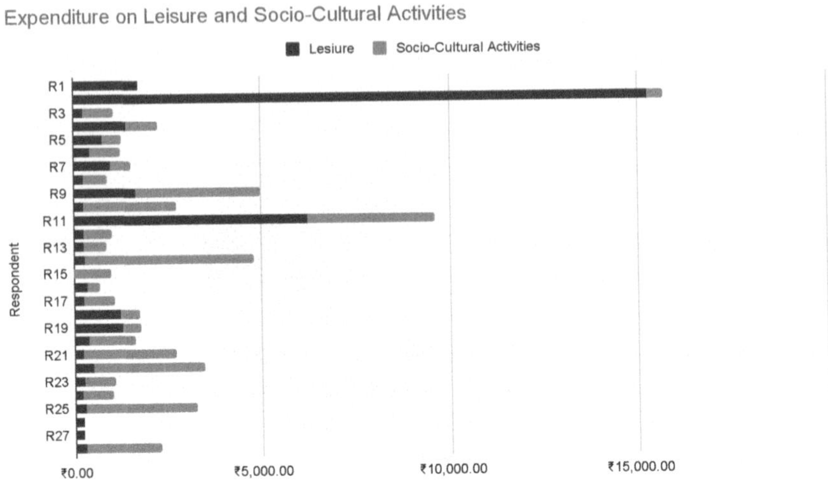

Fig. 6 Month-wise spending on leisure and socio-cultural matters

2250 per month per household. This only covers approximately 7% of their spending (Fig. 7).

4.3 *Gender Polarity*

The interactions with women in the fishing trade opened several new channels of thought. One of the most striking observations was that when asked about daily wages, almost all men responded with 'undetermined'. However, women could explain the nuances of their income and consumption patterns. Upon further inspection, it was discovered that fisherwomen work tirelessly to manage their household finances. All respondents report that at the end of each day, the family's total income is deposited with women (wives for older fishermen and mothers for the youth), who take care of the budget. Decisions on how to spend the received income on household needs, including leisure and cultural spending, are in the hands of these women. Meanwhile, men manage the finances needed for fishing-related activities.

Evidently, while fishing as trade is often associated with men embodying bellicose characteristics, women play an undeniable, and often undervalued, role in the smooth functioning of the supply chain (FAO,

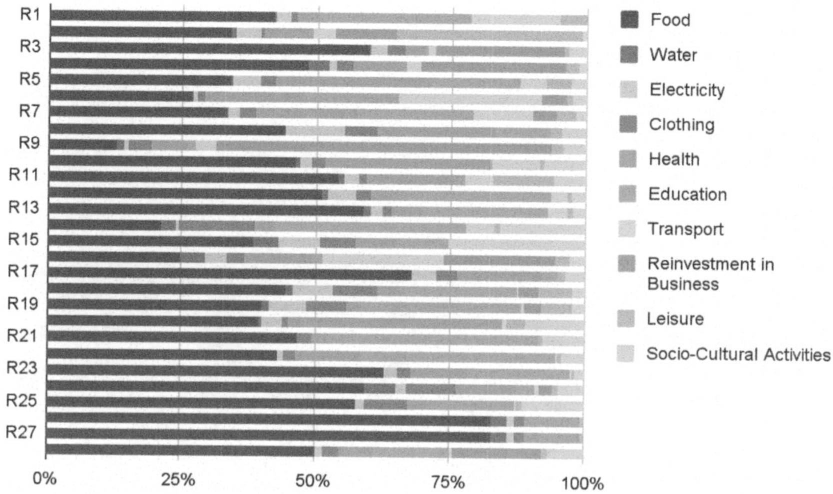

Fig. 7 Month-wise breakdown of the total expenditure

2020). From auction sites to market spaces and door-to-door sales, women actively engage in all aspects except procuring. Going into the sea has been non-verbally 'assigned' as a male role, while women are confined to shore-based activities. Fisherwomen's work being undermined is a symptom of an established gender-based hierarchical system and designated roles that relegate women to underpaid labour and invisibility (Crompton, 2001; Reskin, 2001; Vyas, 2021). Fisherwomen often dwell in the lower socio-economic strata of society. Not only do they have to pay the price of surviving harsh conditions and economic challenges, but they also face resistance due to their gender identity (Image 4). The central statistics have not categorised women under their official tally for full-time 'marine fishers', further propagating this gendered view (Handbook on Fisheries Statistics, 2020).

While the men learn the tricks of the trade from their fathers, women who are either part of or married into these families are left to learn by themselves. They are required not only to know the best prices but also to manage time and juggle both family commitments and work. With no consistent 'workplace' or schedule, women are constantly expected to move and adapt as the demand and supply for fish fluctuate. Even though women manage money and make monetary decisions in the household,

Image 4 A fisherwoman at the shore (Photograph by Jignesh Mistry)

their 'independence' is limited. For instance, in case of emergencies, it is the women's assets which are liquified to support the household. Jewellery pawning is a common occurrence in these parts. The generational wealth, usually passed on to ensure a woman's personal financial security, is sold at informal sites and at very low rates. Thereby, goods meant to provide a sense of autonomy remain at the disposal of household needs and requirements, with women having little to no say in pawning decisions.

As nurturers, women are always taught to put their family's needs first. So, when the need for money does arise, as a part of her upbringing, she is expected to make sacrifices for the well-being of the family as opposed to her own. Like clockwork, the nurturing role begins as she wakes up at 2 A.M., an hour or so earlier than her husband, to cook and ends only when she retires to bed. While juggling between their work at auction sites and marketplaces, they have to take up caregiving duties at home for both the youngins and the old folks. Age, as a dimension, also impacts how fisherwomen experience life. While younger women return back from the marketplaces to wrap up household chores around 2 P.M., the older ones continue to monitor sales until 8–9 P.M. From cooking and cleaning to ensuring water and sanitation facilities and making sure their children are well-groomed, women are expected to manage it all. Borrowing from Betty Friedan's concept of the *Feminine Mystique,* this 'double burden' leads to them being overworked and undervalued (Friedan, 1963).

Fisherwomen's dependency, coupled with the nurturing role which they are boxed into, leads them to live in a state of constant fear. These trepidations have been exacerbated due to the ongoing climate crisis. During the course of this research, most fisherwomen spoke candidly about the psychological distress caused by the uncertainties inherent to the trade. Their growing anxieties about devastating environmental catastrophes, such as tsunami, lead them to invest more in their children's education and encourage them to explore other avenues of work, even if they have to put their assets at stake or take loans.

4.4 Youth Participation (or Lack Thereof)

Education,[5] the developmental tool associated with upward mobility for those from low-income backgrounds, acts as a double-edged sword in the fishing trade (Lin, 2020; Savarimuthu, 1977). At an individual level, the children of fisherfolk are getting educated at higher grades and switching to more secure livelihoods, much to the relief of their families. Collectively, however, the fishing industry is being run by the older folks as the youth are hesitant to join the trade, directly affecting the continuity of it as a generational practice.

Figure 8 shows the education level of the older fishers in the sample (from ages 30 to 57), more than half of whom have not studied past the grade 5 level. From the 30 interviews, it was found that 20% of fisherfolk had no formal education, 44% attended grades 1–5, 20% attended grades 6–8, and 16% graduated from high school. However, almost all children of fisherfolk families have been educated till the undergraduate level. The increased investment and focus on their children's education could have stemmed from the lack of opportunities they had, leading them to take up fishing as a trade.

[5] Education here refers to attending formal establishments such as schools and other higher educational institutions.

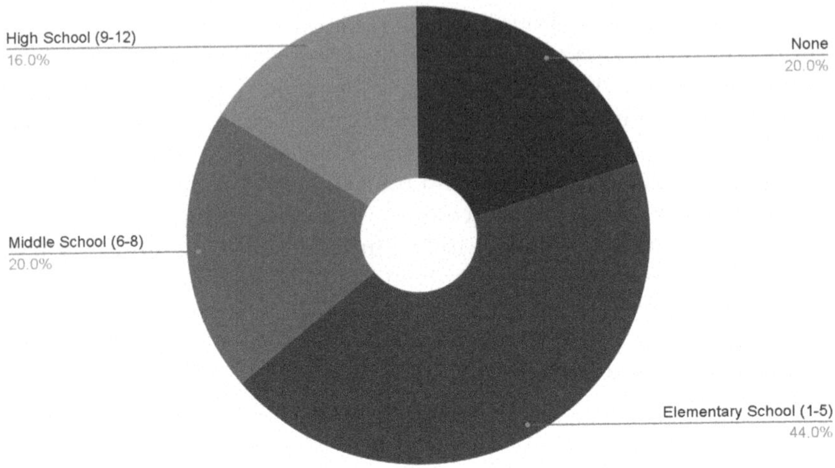

Fig. 8 Education levels of fishers from age 30–57

As per Fig. 9, the youth report working in sectors exclusive to the fishing industry and in geographical locations further away from the coasts. However, some have to fish, not by choice but by compulsion. The reasons for this are twofold; firstly, some youth recognise their importance in the complex food production chain and are sympathetic to the needs of numerous stakeholders dependent on them. For instance, one of the interviewees commented, 'We have to go to the sea and the market every day because if one person goes to the sea, four people will eat that day'. Secondly, due to the dearth of other opportunities, 26.2% of the respondents are forced to resort to fishing, either as full-time or part-time work, to make ends meet.

On the contrary, the sample reports that around 52.4% of males either pursue education or work in other areas. 21.3% of respondents who are married are exclusively women from fisher households. They were wedded right after graduation or before, in some cases, without being given a chance to pursue their job aspirations.

The growing trend of youth withdrawing from fishing pushes the community deeper into the vicious cycle of trade deterioration. Despite technological advancements, the fishers have still not incorporated all the tools available for their assistance. This is because of the following three reasons: most older fisherfolk are not technologically sound, there is a lack

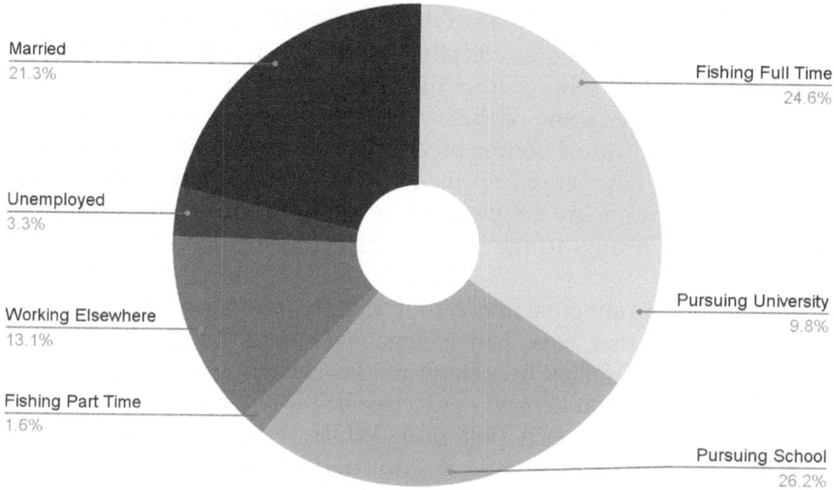

Fig. 9 Current trends in the youth of fisher families (*Note* 'Unemployed' here, refers to an individual who is willing and able to work but is unable to find it.)

of youth participation, and the selling prices of these tools are exorbitant. GPS systems needed for deep-sea navigation are not being extensively used in these parts owing to older fisherfolks' aversion to the risky waters. The pressures of deep-sea fishing, thus, fall on the rapidly declining youth population in the trade.

Additionally, the act of fishing remains highly dependent on manual labour and indigenous knowledge, further reducing youth involvement. This knowledge that has been passed over generations is increasingly losing relevance owing to the growing uncertainties in the wake of the climate crisis.

4.5 Climate Crisis and Marine Pollution

Climate change and erratic weather have a dismal effect on seafaring and navigation. The recent environmental conditions, especially those of winds and tides, do not match or follow the natural patterns maintained over so many years (Srikanthan, 2013). This creates an additional economic burden in buying new equipment and advanced navigation systems like that of the deep-sea GPS, mentioned previously. Additionally, as the sea gets more unpredictable by the day, the mental burden lies heavy atop fishermen who venture into the sea and the ones who are left behind on the shore. Some of these qualms were echoed during an interview when the individual commented, 'My husband has been trapped in cyclones twice. I have stayed up many nights crying, thinking about his safety. I do not want my family to be subjected to this fear again'. The growing anxiety related to the climate crisis has left the fisher families in grave distress.

Alongside environmental uncertainties, there have been several anthropogenic markers that have had a negative impact on the waters, the coasts and fisher families by extension. For instance, tourism, a flourishing industry in Pondicherry and coastal Tamil Nadu, is the leading cause of marine and beach pollution. While visiting the once pristine beaches, one can witness plastic, a grim mascot of the Anthropocene,[6] littered across the length of the coast. Along with waste disposed of by tourists, plastic-based fibres like monofilaments and nylon are present in fishing equipment such as nets (Image 5). These can be traced even at great depths of 4869–5766 m in the waters with concentrations as high as 2000 per m^3 (Fischer et al., 2015). The increase in plastic-dependent fishing equipment can be traced back to the advent of great acceleration, in the early 1960s, where net production was sourced through plastic manufacturers to cut costs and increase effectiveness (Radhalekshmy & Gopalan Nayar, 1973).

The exponential increase in plastic use is reflected in the over 4 billion fibre per square kilometre waste that plagues the Indian Ocean, where most of these SSFs fish (Woodall et al. 2014). Today, the majority of the plastic waste at the beach comprises water bottles, single-use bags, tarpaulin and lost or abandoned fishing gear. Mounds of plastic waste are detangled from fishing nets daily and collected on the shores. Respondents add, as of late, they are catching more plastic than fish in their

[6] The 'Anthropocene' (anthropos meaning man and -cene meaning recent) refers to the proposition that mankind has managed to 'guide' and alter the functioning of the Earth Systems has led to the acknowledgement of a new geological epoch. It grapples with the idea that humans are at the forefront of ecological, geological and socio-political changes. There are various known markers of this human-led epoch such as radionuclides, fly ash particles, aluminium and plastic.

Image 5 Fishers separating plastic from the nets at Kuruchikuppam Village in Puducherry (Photograph by Jignesh Mistry)

nets. This costs the fishers their time and additional unwanted investments for repair. Another major contributor to marine pollution is the sewage pipelines that dispose of waste directly into the sea. The untreated hazardous waste from the states of Tamil Nadu and Puducherry released into the sea causes dire effects on the marine ecosystem (Van Cauwenberghe & Janssen, 2014). This, combined with overfishing, threatens the fish composition in the area (Ojea et al., 2020).

The exploitation of marine species for the benefit of the consumers can nudge them into the endangered/extinct category. In fact, the ongoing Anthropocene epoch has been notoriously described as 'a story about extinctions' by the coveted ecologist Erle Ellis (Anthes, 2016). Scientific explorations show that since humans have entered the evolutionary horizon, the extinction rates have increased by 100–1000 times (De Vos et al. 2015). To avoid the repercussions of the ongoing sixth mass extinction on the fishing industry, the governments of Tamil Nadu and Puducherry have introduced a two-month fishing ban period as a preemptive measure. Beginning from 15 April, fishers are not permitted to venture into the sea until 15 June. This period has been chosen after carefully considering the copulation and birth period of the fish. The only exemption for this ban is fishers using small fibre boats for seafaring, who are allowed to work during specific time periods.

While the ban is imperative for protecting the marine ecosystem, it extends the gap between the nature-human dichotomy. What is a respite for fish turns out to be a period of an intensive economic and mental burden on the fishing communities as they received only Rs 5500 per household for the 61 days. This is an outcome of the under-planned ban measures taken by the state government. This annual low productivity period, whose magnitude worsens each year, drives the fisherfolk to earn lower incomes as living becomes expensive. It is a lose-lose situation as, in the long run, species extinction threatens their incomes. However, in the short run, the ban period severely deteriorates their standard of living—making the dominoes of shocks inescapable.

4.6 Tsunami and/vs. Pandemic

Shocks, at all levels, indiscriminately affect the fisherfolk, who depend on supply and demand-based daily wages. On 26th December 2004, at 7:58 A.M., an unprecedented earthquake of 9.8 magnitudes rose as a tsunami on the unsuspecting locals of Marina Beach. What is now known as the Boxing Day Tsunami sparked an ex-post mechanism of a comprehensive early-tsunami warning system in India, making it the first country to have such an elaborate alarm in place (Bose, 2021). The devastating aftermath of the incident took away the lives of countless people and marine wildlife. The tsunami was a local, supply-side shock, specifically affecting those dwelling on the coast whose houses and business infrastructure were swept away. The recovery was also concentrated, and the local government helped the targeted communities rehabilitate quickly. For instance, fisherfolk whose homes were destroyed during the tsunami were later given permanent rehabilitation at the Tsunami Quarters in Tamil Nadu and Puducherry.

Many fishers have still not moved out of this space owing to economic pressures that come with getting a rented/owned place, like taking sizable loans and paying recurring rents. This highlights the long-term negative impacts of the tsunami. For a considerable number of fisher families, the business investments have still not gone back to the pre-tsunami era, yielding negative returns. The lack of well-equipped fishing gear has had an adverse effect on their ability to venture into the sea, catch a good quantity of fish and sustain themselves. This, in turn, has led them to procure loans (especially informal) and also pawn jewellery to make ends meet at both household and trade levels (Image 6).

Unlike the tsunami recovery that was unique to the community, the COVID-19 pandemic, a health crisis that took the world by storm between 2020 and 2022, was an aggregate shock, affecting each individual across the globe in some capacity. Being both a supply and demand-side shock, the pandemic negatively impacted the market and sales as procurement was low and demand was negligible. With economic structures worldwide coming to a halt, concentrated welfare measures were not considered a feasible policy. Adding on, fishing is ultimately a cog in the primary good procurement machine, and systems were not in place to combat fishers' specific vulnerabilities. The government-mandated spatial and time-wise regulations on sea visits heavily limited the fisherfolk's income.

At the offset of the pandemic, especially during the first and second waves, the Central Government of India had forbidden fishers to venture

Image 6 A boy walks past the Tsunami Sea Deity Statue at Vaithikuppam Village, Puducherry (Photograph by Jignesh Mistry)

into the sea and assemble at the market sites, rendering them helpless with no means of disposable income. Several interviewees also reported instances of being chased by police officers in their frail attempts to catch fish and sell them at the beach. Some fisherfolk also formed collectives to raise their concerns to the municipal office and the Tamil Nadu and Puducherry governments. They argued that if their counterparts, i.e. farmers, were allowed to continue crop cultivation, they should have had the same opportunities. Eventually, as the fishing restrictions eased, the fishermen were allowed to venture into the sea for a mere two hours. Subsequently, fisherwomen spent the next two hours attempting to sell the yield while facing several hurdles. The marketplaces were deserted owing to the mobility restrictions imposed, affecting their already hampered incomes.

While the entire world is trying to recover from the grave repercussions of the pandemic, the SSFs have arguably been more vulnerable than some others. The SSFs from India often come from lower caste and class backgrounds, making them more susceptible to being alienated from mitigation and adaptation strategies. With their lives and livelihoods threatened, the business model for SSFs has completely changed through the pandemic and its recovery period. There has been a significant increase in door-to-door sales as markets closed and yield could no longer be pooled at auction sites. Even with the markets and auction sites reopening, the footfall in these spaces has reduced, which could also imply dietary modifications in the community. However, the silver lining is that the inevitable break from fishing provided some time and space for the marine ecosystem to rejuvenate, which would benefit SSFs in the long run (Jigeesh, 2020; John, 2020, as cited in Bennett et al., 2020).

Evidently, the SSF community is vulnerable to unprecedented stressors because of their socio-economic position in society. While fisherfolk were still in the midst of building their lives and livelihoods that were lost during the 2004 tsunami, the ongoing COVID-19 health crisis became an added stressor. While both cases had different implications, the crux remains that these communities need concentrated preparedness policy measures to protect them from facing the brunt of such unexpected conditions.

5 Conclusion

History repeats itself in the lack of ex-ante prevention measures post the 2004 tsunami. The devastating after-effects of the calamity highlighted the weak social and infrastructural setups of the fishing industry. Ex-post measures, such as the Tsunami Quarters and early-tsunami warning systems, were installed, and monetary relief was handed out. In the long term, however, uncertainty still remains. The coasts of Tamil Nadu and Puducherry are not any less prone to environmental and other shocks now than it was a vicennium ago; the risks and subsequent vulnerability have only increased.

The human-nature dichotomy prevails in how policy and relief measures are designed and implemented. Recognising the intrinsic cyclical and dialectic synergy between the environment and civilisation is imperative. As much as an environmental catastrophe is a disaster, several added socio-economic shocks have made the lives and livelihoods of SSFs vulnerable in the long term. For instance, losing their residence translates to the loss of social networks built over the years, the little savings they had gathered for substantial investments, and most importantly, some financial stability they had secured with generations of hard work. Looking at the lives of fisherfolk through the solitary lenses of the issues discussed would be incomplete. With this research, the overworked and underpaid nature of this trade has come to light.

Devoid of steady incomes, fisherfolk are forced to build their lives around their variable, meagre income. The month-wise expenditure that the households incur just to procure essential services is not in tandem with their earnings, causing them to take loans from formal and informal sources. One of the biggest credit sources is jewellery pawn shops, which take away an important personal financial asset of women of fisher households. In addition to a lack of autonomy, fisherwomen are burdened with all house-related chores and fish sales. Their serving and nurturing role, both at home and outside, limits them from venturing into the sea along with their male counterparts, thus reducing the essential manpower needed in the industry.

The number of individuals motivated to join the fishing trade is reducing steeply. Most youth from fisher families are inclined towards finding other jobs that promise a steady income stream. This has led fisher parents to invest exponentially more in education, even at the cost of borrowing money, to help them escape the generational cycle of trade-related distress. However, some are forced to return back to the trade due to a dearth of alternative opportunities. The youth entering the industry bring with them the knowledge of modern technology needed to cope with the environmental changes that the seasoned fisherfolk are unfamiliar with.

Plastics and marine pollution have exacerbated the already challenging nature of the trade. Increased single-use plastic, along with improved tourism, has flooded these parts with non-biodegradable waste, hindering fishers' work. Changing tides and winds have made it difficult to navigate through the sea based on the indigenous knowledge that fishers had. This, coupled with the disaster-prone nature of this area, has adversely affected their lives and livelihoods. Fisherfolk are forced to seek help only when disasters strike, even though they face daily distress.

The use of feminist ethnographic methodology facilitated the reflection on socio-economic and environment dynamics of a vulnerable space. Our approach, inherently feminist, prioritised an exploration of the industry, gender dynamics and power relations, with a deep commitment to amplifying the often-overlooked voices of women within these communities. Through interdisciplinary collusion, as well as collaborating with a myriad of stakeholders in the study, we got a chance to weave diverse perspectives and unpack the multitude of complexities at play. Integrating polyvocality also ensured we did not rely excessively on a singular voice and did justice to the rich tapestry of experiences within the fishing communities. The diverse group of participants added depth and authenticity to our research, ensuring that our narrative did not fall into the trap of hyper-generalisation. Overall, this study underscores the power of collaboration, polyvocality and feminist ethnographic inquiry in shedding light on the lives, struggles and resilience of the fishing communities in Tamil Nadu and Puducherry.

References

Anthes, E. (2016, October 11). Are Humans Creating More Species Than We're Killing? *The Atlantic*. https://www.theatlantic.com/science/archive/2016/10/human-speciation/503597/

Arksey, H., & Knight, P. (1999). *Interviewing for Social Scientists*. SAGE. https://doi.org/10.4135/9781849209335

Banerjee, A., & Duflo, E. (2011). *Poor Economics: A Radical Rethinking of the Way to Fight Global Poverty* (Reprint edition). PublicAffairs.

Bennett, N. J., Finkbeiner, E. M., Ban, N. C., Belhabib, D., Jupiter, S. D., Kittinger, J. N., Mangubhai, S., Scholtens, J., Gill, D., & Christie, P. (2020). The COVID-19 Pandemic, Small-Scale Fisheries and Coastal Fishing Communities. *Coastal Management, 48*(4), 336–347. https://doi.org/10.1080/08920753.2020.1766937

Bose, J. (2021, December 26). 2004 Indian Ocean Tsunami: 17 Years on, a Look Back at One of the Deadliest Natural Disasters in History. *Hindustan Times*. https://www.hindustantimes.com/world-news/2004-indian-ocean-tsunami-17-years-on-a-look-back-at-one-of-the-deadliest-natural-disasters-in-history-101640476494667.html

Building Back Better For Our Children. (2006). United Nations Team for Tsunami Recovery Support. https://www.preventionweb.net/files/2150_VL323100.pdf.

Cánovas-Molina, A., & García-Frapolli, E. (2022). A Review of Vulnerabilities in Worldwide Small-Scale Fisheries. *Fisheries Management and Ecology, 29*(5), 491–501. https://doi.org/10.1111/fme.12538

Coulthard, S., Mcgregor, J. A., & White, C. S. (2018). Chapter 15: Multiple Dimensions of Wellbeing in Practice. In K. Schreckenberg, G. Mace, & M. Poudyal (Eds.), *Ecosystem Services and Poverty Alleviation: Trade-Offs and Governance* (pp. 243–256). Routledge.

Crompton, R. (2001). Social Class and Gender. In N. J. Smelser & P. B. Baltes (Eds.), *International Encyclopedia of the Social & Behavioral Sciences* (pp. 14233–14238). Pergamon. https://doi.org/10.1016/B0-08-043076-7/04000-6

De Vos, J. M., Joppa, L. N., Gittleman, J. L., Stephens, P. R., & Pimm, S. L. (2015). Estimating the Normal Background Rate of Species Extinction. *Conservation Biology, 29*(2), 452–462. https://doi.org/10.1111/cobi.12380

Economic Survey 2020–21 (Vol. 1). (2021). Government of India. https://www.indiabudget.gov.in/economicsurvey/ebook_es2021/index.html#p=616

FAO. (2020). The Impact of COVID-19 on Fisheries and Aquaculture Food Systems. Possible Responses—Information Paper, November 2020: Information Paper, November 2020. FAO. https://doi.org/10.4060/cb2537en

Fischer, V., Elsner, N. O., Brenke, N., Schwabe, E., & Brandt, A. (2015). Plastic Pollution of the Kuril-Kamchatka Trench Area (NW Pacific). *Deep Sea Research Part II: Topical Studies in Oceanography, 111*, 399–405. https://doi.org/10.1016/j.dsr2.2014.08.012

Friedan, B. (1963). *The Feminine Mystique*. Norton.

Gander, P., van den Berg, M., & Signal, L. (2009). Sleep and Sleepiness of Fishermen on Rotating Schedules. *Chronobiology International, 25*(2), 389–398. https://doi.org/10.1080/07420520802106728

Handbook of Fisheries Statistics, 2020. (2020). [Government Report]. Department of Fisheries, Ministry of Fisheries, Animal Husbandry & Dairying, Government of India. https://dof.gov.in/sites/default/files/2021-02/Final_Book.pdf

Islam, Md. M., Sallu, S., Hubacek, K., & Paavola, J. (2013). Vulnerability of Fishery-Based Livelihoods to the Impacts of Climate Variability and Change: Insights from Coastal Bangladesh. *Regional Environmental Change, 14*(1), 281–294. https://doi.org/10.1007/s10113-013-0487-6

Jigeesh, A. M. (2020, April 13). *Distressed Fisheries Sector Demands Immediate Support* [The Hindu BuisnessLine]. https://www.thehindubusinessline.com/economy/agri-business/distressed-fisheries-sector-demands-immediate-support/article31332857.ece

John, H. (2020, January 2). *Fish Meal and Fish Oil Industries Pose Threat to the Fishing Sector in India*. Mongabay. https://india.mongabay.com/2020/01/fish-meal-and-fish-oil-industries-pose-threat-to-the-fishing-sector-in-india/

Lin, M. (2020). Educational Upward Mobility. Practices of Social Changes—Research on Social Mobility and Educational Inequality. *International Journal of Social Science Studies, 8*(3), Article 3. https://doi.org/10.11114/ijsss.v8i3.4789

Matthew, A. (2015). *Small-Scale Fisheries (SSF) in India*. United Nations. https://www.un.org/depts/los/nippon/unnff_programme_home/unnff_programme_sg_report/AnsyMatthew_Small-scale_fisheries.pdf

Medic, G., Wille, M., & Hemels, M. E. (2017). Short- and Long-term Health Consequences of Sleep Disruption. *Nature and Science of Sleep, 9*, 151–161. https://doi.org/10.2147/NSS.S134864

Noman, M. A. A., Sharmin, T., Shoshi, F. K., Sanjida, Anee, K. F., Hossain, M. B., Islam, M. N., & Khan, M. S. I. (2020). Occupational Hazards and Health Care Seeking Behavior of Fishermen. *Asian Journal of Medical and Biological Research, 6*(1), Article 1. https://doi.org/10.3329/ajmbr.v6i1.46477

Ojea, E., Lester, S. E., & Salgueiro-Otero, D. (2020). Adaptation of Fishing Communities to Climate-Driven Shifts in Target Species. *One Earth, 2*(6), 544–556. https://doi.org/10.1016/j.oneear.2020.05.012

Patro, S., Sahu, B., & Pati, B. K. (2020). Food Consumption Pattern and Nutrient Intake by the Fishermen Community of Ganjam District, Odisha. *International Journal of Current Microbiology and Applied Sciences, 9*(12), 672–680. https://doi.org/10.20546/ijcmas.2020.912.081

Radhalekshmy, K., & Gopalan Nayar, S. (1973). Synthetic Fibres for Fishing Gear. *Fishery Technology, 10*(2), 142–165.

Reskin, B. F. (2001). Sex Segregation at Work. In N. J. Smelser & P. B. Baltes (Eds.), *International Encyclopedia of the Social & Behavioral Sciences* (pp. 13962–13965). Pergamon. https://doi.org/10.1016/B0-08-043076-7/03994-2

Savarimuthu, S. (1977). *Education and Social Mobility in Tamil Nadu, India: An Empirical Study of Intergenerational Occupational Mobility and Occupational Aspiration* [PhD Dissertation, Loyola University Chicago]. https://ecommons.luc.edu/luc_diss/1745

Srikanthan, S. (2013). Impact of Climate Change on the Fishermen's Livelihood Development: A Case Study of Village in Coromandel Coast. *IOSR Journal of Humanities and Social Science, 12*(6), 49–54. https://doi.org/10.9790/0837-1264954

The Wild Life (Protection) Act, 1972 (1972). https://legislative.gov.in/sites/default/files/A1972-53_0.pdf

Umamaheswari, T., Sugumar, G., Krishnan, P., Ananthan, P. S., Anand, A., Jeevamani, J. J. J., Mahendra, R. S., Amali Infantina, J., & Srinivasa Rao, C. (2021). Vulnerability Assessment of Coastal Fishing Communities for Building Resilience and Adaptation: Evidences from Tamil Nadu, India. *Environmental Science & Policy, 123*, 114–130. https://doi.org/10.1016/j.envsci.2021.05.009

Van Cauwenberghe, L., & Janssen, C. R. (2014). Microplastics in Bivalves Cultured for Human Consumption. *Environmental Pollution, 193*, 65–70. https://doi.org/10.1016/j.envpol.2014.06.010

Vyas, N. (2021). Undermining the Role of Women in the Economy: The Interplay Between Paid Work and Unpaid Care Work in India. *Industrial Law Journal*. https://doi.org/10.1093/indlaw/dwab035

Woodall, L. C., Sanchez-Vidal, A., Canals, M., Paterson, G. L. J., Coppock, R., Sleight, V., Calafat, A., Rogers, A. D., Narayanaswamy, B. E., & Thompson, R. C. (2014). The Deep Sea is a Major Sink for Microplastic Debris. *Royal Society Open Science, 1*(4). https://doi.org/10.1098/rsos.140317

Zacharia, P. U., Ap, D., Thomas, S., Kizhakudan, S., Vivekanandan, E., Pillai, L., Sivadas, M., Ghosh, S., U, G., K M, R., Nair, R., Najmudeen, T., Koya, M., Chellappan, A., Dash, G., Divipala, I., Akhilesh, K. V., Menon, M., & Sen, S. (2016). *Relative Vulnerability Assessment of Indian Marine Fishes to Climate Change using Impact and Adaptation Attributes*. CMFRI Special Publication 125. https://www.researchgate.net/publication/311237426_Relative_vulnerability_assessment_of_Indian_marine_fishes_to_climate_change_using_impact_and_adaptation_attributes

CHAPTER 4

Flooding Urbanity: Narratives from *Safai Karamcharis* of Guwahati, Assam

Ashika Thomas, Sakshi Chindaliya, Deepanshu Mohan, and Rishiraj Sen

Abstract Post the devastating floods of Assam in 2022, a team of ethnographers took to the streets of the capital city Guwahati to explore the turbulent hydro-social dynamics. This paper is a documentation of

D. Mohan
Centre for New Economics Studies, Jindal School of Liberal Arts and Humanities, O.P. Jindal Global University, Sonipat, India
e-mail: dmohan@jgu.edu.in

A. Thomas (✉)
London School of Economics and Political Science, London, England
e-mail: ashikathms@gmail.com

S. Chindaliya · D. Mohan
Jindal School of Liberal Arts and Humanities, O.P Jindal Global University, Sonipat, India
e-mail: sakshichindaliya@yahoo.in

R. Sen
Indian Institute of Management Ahmedabad, Ahmedabad, India
e-mail: senrishiraj28@gmail.com

D. Mohan et al. (eds.), *Pan-India Stories of Informal Workers During Covid-19 Pandemic*, https://doi.org/10.1007/978-981-97-1525-1_4

the hidden narrative of sanitation workers in the slums of Guwahati; a community doomed to cater to the needs of the urban collective over their own. It delves into the nuances of caste and gender dimensions that govern the fragile livelihoods of the community most vulnerable to floods in the region—safai karamcharis. The study explores the undertones of informality in a formal work set-up and the cyclical nature of the annual disaster. The observations and analysis from this project add to (Coulthard et al. in Ecosystem Services and Poverty Alleviation: Trade-offs and Governance, Routledge, 2018) Multidimensionality of Poverty by expanding the definition of ecosystem services and its implications at the community level.

1 Introduction

"We will not be able to travel far in this weather, Guwahati is our only choice as a field site." It was late July of 2022, at the peak of monsoons, when we were in conversation with a field ethnographer, Rishi, who is a resident of Assam and was hoping to contextualize his experience with the catastrophic floods through a research project. Much like an annual tradition, the ferocious (overflowing) waters of Barak and Brahmaputra wreaked havoc in the state. To make matters worse, Rishi noted that human actions (or lack thereof), such as unplanned urban growth, rapid deforestation, hill cutting, encroachments along embankments, and lack of proper drainage systems, among others, also made urban Guwahati more susceptible to flooding.

"Honestly, all things considered, everyone had foreseen the flood, but they did not anticipate its grave magnitude. I mean, that's why it is receiving wide media coverage." To investigate further, we spent the next few minutes going through articles in the news to map stakeholder narratives; it seemed to begin with municipal officers and end with upper and middle-class urban dwellers. In recounting his experiences, Rishi offhandedly mentioned the overflowing drainage system. Out of curiosity, we inquired about the management of drainage systems in the capital city of Assam. Rishi, who was aware of Guwahati's sanitation channels, informed us that they were cleaned by safai karamcharis (Hindi term for sanitation workers) who resided in the Harijan colonies located (to our surprise) at the heart of the city. Despite this, there wasn't a single mention of them in the context of the crisis, which they were equally, if not more, vulnerable to.

Back in the day, silt-rich floods used to bring with them a promise of a bountiful harvest to floodplains like that of Assam, a direct contrast to its erosive nature today. Assam has an Overall (flood) Vulnerability Index Score of 0.616, the highest in the country (Mohanty & Wadhawan, 2021).[1] The most recent spate of the 2022 Assam floods once again alerted the nation to the devastating repercussions of such a calamity, while also bringing it to the forefront of mainstream media and academic scrutiny. The flood has affected close to 9 million people and took over 195 lives throughout the state (Times of India, 2022). Despite being the frontline responders in combating urban floods, *Safai Karamcharis* were undervalued and underappreciated in this discourse. This was not uncommon elsewhere in the country either, as those belonging to the lower strata of society are forced to work in emergencies and are continuously left to fend for themselves during a crisis.

"*Safai karamchari*" or sanitation worker, according to the National Commission for Safai Karamcharis Act, 1993, refers to a "person engaged in, or employed for, manually carrying human excreta or any sanitation work." In India, these duties are relegated to the lower caste communities. Among the four main tiers of this occupation-based, archaic Hindu belief, sanitation workers fall into the lowest one—the *Dalits*. The Hindu caste system, which has existed since the Brahmanical period (circa 1100–500 BCE), is a form of social stratification based on the notion of purity and pollution. It has five primary groups:

- Brahmins, those who assumed authoritative and intellectual positions,
- Kshatriyas, the warrior faction,
- Vaishyas, those who controlled the markets,
- Shudras, those termed as "unskilled workers," including peasants and servants, and
- Dalits, known as "untouchables," were shunned as not being worthy of caste status (Singh, 2016).

The caste system is an endogamous ancestral hierarchy that has left limited opportunities for those with the short end of the stick. While

[1] The authors have devised a climate vulnerability index for India which is calculated by using the formula Vulnerability(f) = (Exposure × Sensitivity)/(Adaptive Capacity). They have analyzed Indian States and Union Territories through time and spatial variation.

revolutionary activists such as Dr. B.R. Ambedkar attempted to dismantle the caste system, the long-drawn history of segregation has affected the country to date. Albeit subtle, the lack of access to resources has forced individuals to succumb to the sub-par conditions that were historically allocated to them due to their caste identities (Jodhka, 2015; Sankaran et al., 2017; Singh, 2016). *Safai karamcharis* is one such homogenous community who are still facing the repercussions of caste-based oppression. In various other sectors in India, there has been inter-caste mobility; however, within the sanitation workforce, it is still stagnant.

Based on our interactions with the community, *Safai Karamcharis* in Guwahati comprise primarily of the Basfore community, who migrated from present-day Bihar and Uttar Pradesh. Categorized as *ati-shudras*, they are compelled to undertake "dirty work." Like other sects in the Dalit sub-group, they are required to maintain cleanliness and capitulate to sanitation roles like brooming, mopping, cleaning toilets and drains, and collecting garbage. The Basfore community is employed by government, semi-government, and private entities on either informal, contractual, or full-time employment basis. Since improper drainage systems are the primary cause of urban floods, sanitation workers in Guwahati are expected to put in extra hours to clean pipelines and dispose of debris. In the process, those working in perilous jobs with limited access to resources face graver risks in terms of loss of lives and livelihoods.

To critically analyze the glaring lack of sanitation workers' experiences during the calamity, we drew inspiration from Coulthard et al.'s (2018) multidimensional well-being concept, especially in its link between poverty, natural circumstances, ecosystems, and service distribution. In a state of emergency such as floods, when the services provided by the community are of the utmost importance, the *safai karamcharis* own well-being is compromised. To understand the nuances of the sanitation workers' experiences during floods, we designed an ethnographic study and implemented it in the city. The survey and interview questionnaire were structured to analyze circumstances apart from their apparent economic conditions. This chapter delves into their lives and livelihoods, exploring the urban spaces sanitation workers reside in, their role in combating floods, the undertones of informality in their formal work, and the undeniable gender polarity.

2 Location

The sanitation workforce in Guwahati comprises a homogenous group; people belonging to the Basfore sub-caste who primarily reside in the Harijan colonies of the urban locale. Barely a glance is spared to their stagnant and seemingly invaluable lives, despite being in the heart of the city and among frequent footfalls. *Safai karamcharis* live a fast-paced life, often rushing from one job to another, paying no mind to the overcast skies and the imminent rain. Residents rushing to work at 8:30 A.M. through the narrow pathways, where Kaccha houses are neatly tucked into rows, is a common sight in the area.

The interconnected lanes of Uzanbazar lead one to a few striking infrastructures—a railway track too close for comfort, a run-down "school," and a single water tap for all its residents. Rupnagar sits across prominent government offices, explaining its marginally better conditions compared to the other areas. Clean drinking water, however, is still scarce. Colonies 3 and 4 being devoid of a name is a precursor to their state of neglect. Landslides are a staple as their homes, roofed with thin plastic, fabric, and tarpaulin, barely hold out against the incessant rains. The hilly regions of Colonies 3 and 4 make it inaccessible for drinking water trucks, much less emergency relief for the landslides that frequent the area. Across all colonies, broken pipelines and overflowing streams result in stagnant waters and destroyed roads.

Nevertheless, the *safai karamcharis* consider this overcrowded space their home as their parents, and forefathers have lived and grown up here. Historically, India has followed a caste-based spatial arrangement, alongside a religious one. While this practice was not state-mandated, it portrayed an unspoken social hierarchy (Bharati et al., 2018; Sahgal et al., 2021; Singh et al., 2019). In Guwahati, however, caste differences are subtle. Individuals from multiple caste orders occupy the same spaces in the city. As one talks to working residents, they repeatedly mention the caste-based nuances present in one's job titles and mannerisms. The Basfores are outcasted and often stereotyped to be heavy alcohol consumers. Members of the Yadav caste, also residents of the same colony, advise not to visit Basfore's personal spaces, *"To be honest, you will gain nothing by going there. Local alcohol is produced there, and people keep drinking that. It's not worthwhile to go."*

Any outsider's presence is immediately met with harsh looks and stern dismissal—a sign of empty unkept promises. The colony residents are reluctant to divulge information, despite the terrible circumstances that befall them due to frequent eviction warnings and visits from government officials. When faced with dislodgement notices, Colony 3's sanitation workers raise pointed questions, *"As it rains and floods constantly and the covid disease is rampant, if the authorities evict us, where will almost 200 or so families in this area go? Where can we live?"* These abysmal conditions remain perennial.

3 Methodology

This feminist ethnographic study stems from a survey conducted in 4 major Harijan Colonies in urban Guwahati. Our team of field researchers visited Uzanbazar, Rupnagar, and Colonies 3 and 4, covering major topographical markers like the steep valleys and the river plains. From a minimal pool of Harijan colonies, these locations were chosen considering their proximity to the ethnographers and their familiarity with the space. An enquiry was set up with the colony members, where 32 sanitation workers and their kin were interviewed by Rishi and his team of ethnographers over the span of a month's time. Due to the pandemic restrictions and road blockages owing to floods, only one preliminary visit to each neighborhood could be conducted.

From the first visit to the last, the entire research team relied upon the on-field ethnographers' lives tied to Guwahati. While engaging in retrospective reflections, we spoke about their working knowledge of the region. We discussed what the first point of contact was like and evaluated how they built networks (of knowledge) in the field. Rishi, the lead on-field ethnographer, commented,

> We knew a bit about the space and the community. While growing up, we were told that in the Harijan colonies (that's what those particular slums were called), mostly sanitation and hygiene workers lived. From that basic understanding, we started to get in touch with organisations representing the communities living there. However, initially, we were only able to build contact in one colony. In one of the other colonies, we went directly inside and asked residents if they would like to talk to us. Our knowledge of Hindi and local languages came in handy. In the third colony, the students my co-ethnographers had previously taught, offered to take us around and introduced us to their families and friends. The most surprising was the final colony we visited, as our point of contact did not turn up at all. A sixteen-year-old boy who was standing outside, heard us talking and kindly

offered to help. He took us to the colony and introduced us to his people. We were then able to go around and interview the community.

A comprehensive questionnaire was built based on these preliminary visits to the community to determine their socio-economic portfolios. The questionnaire building was coordinated between the project team present across different parts of the country and Rishi and his team on ground in Guwahati. The conversations after the preliminary recce and several rigorous brainstorming sessions led us to develop a questionnaire that gauged the community's added vulnerabilities to external short and long-term shocks such as the annual floods and the COVID-19 pandemic. While it was made to be holistic in nature, Rishi mentioned that he had to alter the questions frequently as each sanitation worker had varying household issues ranging from chronic illnesses to turbulent community life. The semi-structured interview format allowed for such individual circumstances to be put forward in a first-person narrative, leaving little to no room for pre-imposed views from the ethnographer's side (Arksey & Knight, 1999). This was especially important considering that Rishi and his team were from the area and were familiar with the general norms and notions of the city's built environment and its residents:

> While this space was "new", at the end of the day, it was still in Guwahati. We have lived here for more than twenty years, and so the challenges were not really challenges- it was our normal. For example, the narrow muddy roads that got littered with garbage thanks to floods (and landslides) have always been part of how we imagine and experience the monsoons. So, these issues, which people might think are the biggest roadblocks in conducting fieldwork, didn't really bother us at all. The real obstacle to overcome, for us, was to provide a safe space for the karamcharis to share openly, considering they have always lived under the fear of authorities and the establishment. To navigate that, we had to talk and joke with them, while trying to build the trust that we weren't going to harm them. The challenge was also posed by the timing, as when we visited, the men were out for work and the women were busy with their household chores. In fact because of the floods and the pandemic, sanitation workers had to take up additional jobs to make ends meet and sustain themselves. As strangers, it was a bit difficult to convince them to talk to us- but that is not to say that it was unachievable, it just took a longer while, given the circumstances.

Owing to the sanitation worker's busy schedules and the erratic weather, we adopted a mixed approach of in-depth interviews and focus groups to gather data. After the first few recorded conversations, we noted that this arrangement allowed the participants to converse freely and delve into personal experiences in multiple settings. Unlike individual interviews, where the responses could not be simultaneously corroborated by the community at large, focus groups helped instantaneously validate individual factual statements such as the drinking water timings and electricity charges (Arksey & Knight, 1999). A limitation of focus groups, though, is the masking of the individual voice and the possibility of group affirmation (Smithson, 2000). This was avoided by the repetition of relevant questions to everyone, which guaranteed their unique responses. Within this seemingly identical group, we attempted to document diverse voices of the connected yet distinct colonies of Guwahati.

Across group and individual interviews, we found that doing ethnography in the backdrop of a dual crisis (flooding during a pandemic) meant that respondents expected solutions for each problem they mentioned. The ethnographers had to think on their feet and maneuver their way through being mistaken for government officials and other policy stakeholders, from whom these solutions were expected. Considering the gravity of the situation, however, there were some instances of resistance on the respondents' part. Rishi recounts,

> In one of the colonies, our point of contact told us to keep it a secret that they helped us enter the area. We distinctly remember that as soon as we arrived, the residents surrounded us, thinking we were government officials who had sent them a notice to vacate the colony a few days ago. They began asking questions like 'Who are you?', 'Where are you from?', 'Who sent you?', and 'Are you with the state authorities?'. We managed it by simply being calm and repeatedly telling them that we were merely students who were doing a study and that we were there to listen to their problems. Some convincing later, they understood and cooperated.
>
> Trusting us to be harmless students, they began opening up about the problems. They highlighted the struggles of living in huge families consisting of both young children and the elderly in congested houses, with no electricity, no drinking water and so on. Some of the participants also repeatedly asked us to visit the government officials and convince them to let the workers stay, emphasizing that they had nowhere to go if they were evicted from the colony- which was their birthplace.

Despite not being foreigners to the place, the ethnographers felt the social gaps, which were exemplified by the resident's behavior toward them. Their dynamic positionality with respect to the respondents changed throughout the course of the project, ultimately leading them to oscillate between being an outsider and an insider. In certain cases, their higher caste and class status being pointed out created a dissonance between the ethnographers and residents. As an attempt to bridge gaps induced by social identities, Rishi and the team adapted by accepting the inductions into the respondent's physical space and actively engaging in their customs at their place of being.

> As much as I didn't want to draw the "us and them" boundaries, the truth is, there were gaps. But these were not as unilateral as one might think. The class-caste-gender intersection played a huge role. One instance that stands out in particular is when we visited a respondent's house and were offered a seat on their bed. We refused since we had gotten consent to film the interview and take photographs of the space. While we did not think much of initially saying no, the young kid who was sitting there previously offered to clean the seat. The caste undertones in the statement, implying the idea of "purity", moved us deeply. As a resolution, we learnt from our experience and made conscious attempts to make amends in the moments and hopefully not find ourselves in similar situations. We promptly seated ourselves close to the child so as to make him comfortable with our presence in his home. In the future, for instance, when we were served lemonade, which was almost always the case, despite being full, we made sure we drank every drop. We wanted to avoid reinforcing caste and class boundaries inadvertently. This incident made us acknowledge our privileges and how our presence affects people...It was tough for us to listen to their problems and yet unable to extend support. We felt helpless, too, just in a different way.

In due process, we had hoped to bridge the gender gap owing to having a balanced gender composition in the team, but this did not work on ground. While men and women in the sample were interviewed separately due to their varying work hours, the team noted that when interviewed as a family or a couple, men dominated the conversation. Despite attempting to create an unhindered setting for the female sanitation workers to open up about the gendered dynamics and domestic issues, we were met with resistance. This led to the information collected on gender polarity during the study being primarily based on the team's detached observations and body language assessment, and not the verbal responses,

> Despite my co-ethnographers identifying as women, it was difficult to establish contact with female sanitation workers. The men were open to talking, whereas it took much convincing from our side to get the women (primarily daughters-in-law) to speak to us. Where the males were not present, only then the women came forward to talk freely…Once, I recall, we approached a female sanitation worker just outside her home and was immediately stopped by her husband demanding why we must speak to her specifically and not to him.

The ethnographic exchange, involving participatory observation, featured in-depth conversations about their (sanitation workers') experiences with floods while also taking a holistic approach and observing their general "wellness" as per Coulthard's framework (2018). The relationship between ecosystem services and poverty, through direct dependence on natural water sources and waste material for survival, complements the analysis of sanitation workers in our sample.[2] By expanding the existing definition of an "ecosystem service" in a community setting to include sanitation work, the stories documented add to the evolving paradigm and highlight the socio-ecological and economic positionality of the people of Guwahati. This study aims to recognize the diversity within the population responsible for the upkeep and maintenance of urban ecosystems, which in turn contribute to the well-being of the city as a whole, especially during a crisis.

4 Observations and Findings

4.1 *"Informality" of Work During Floods*

The daily hustle-bustle of *safai karamcharis* in Guwahati is constant, come rain or shine. Despite being one of the primary stakeholders in stopping diseases from spreading in cities, sanitation workers do not experience job satisfaction and security. They are underpaid and overburdened under the garb of menial work. To their credit, the government provides marginally better working conditions and a base salary of Rs.

[2] Ecosystem services refer to basic sustenance mechanisms provided by or extracted from nature, including, but not limited to, food, water, air, etc.

8000. Considering the worker's tenure and their unabated service in the sanitation space, they may even get remuneration as high as Rs. 38,000 per month. However, more often than not, sanitation workers in Guwahati are hired on a contractual basis. Women, especially, are employed this way since they work primarily at the household level. *Safai karamcharis* receive monthly payments based on the successful completion of their tasks and are forced to report to work even during heavy floods.

In India, the formal workspace is complemented by steady pay, insurance benefits and several detailed perks. Meanwhile, work in the informal sector is characterized by inter-generational skills learnt outside of the formal training systems present in the country (Basole, 2014; Gammarano & Kapsos, 2018; Sheikh & Gaurav, 2020). Sanitation work can be classified as both without entirely belonging to either, qualifying it as a blindspot for employment and livelihood policies. Betwixt and between, they are exposed to unfair wage cuts and assigned duties outside the purview of their drafted contracts. One of the few designated roles in the space is that of wet and dry waste collection, assigned to men and women, respectively. However, "during the Monsoons, the distinction vanishes in flooded urban alleys" (Harriss-White, 2017).

Unlike formal work centered in a singular space, the whole city becomes a site of intervention for the *safai karamcharis*. As drains span across the urban landscape, juggling between these "workplaces" while (trying to) combat intensive flooding carries its specific challenges. With the ever-rising water sitting still atop the roads, navigating through it knee-deep causes turbulence and impedes the completion of tasks. M. Basfore questioned, "*There was so much water this time. How will I go to work?*" Flooding reduces visibility and makes individuals more susceptible to getting hurt. D. Basfore, a sanitation worker from Colony 4, commented, "*When it rains, my mother has difficulty going to work. She has to go despite the rainfall....There are landslides too.*"

Adding to the mobility issues, the situation is made worse by a dearth of proper equipment that should be allocated to sanitation workers. The two coconut leaves brooms, the only equipment provided by the government, are notably insufficient to fulfill their daily duties. Several interviewees commented on having to locate junk and scraps to manufacture tools to aid the cleaning process. They are forced to create unreliable contraptions using a hammer on malleable tin sheets, which are then loosely attached to a stick—compelling *safai karamcharis* to test the odds with each use. Any additional costs for ensuring safety were made out of pocket. Despite the risks involved, sanitation workers pick up their make-shift toolkits to fulfill their job requirements. Even though the group is unionized at almost 90% across the country, the insufficient municipal budget stops them from receiving the much-needed protective equipment and health insurance (Harriss-White, 2017) (Image 1).

Banished to the bottom of the barrel, they are expected to survive on the scraps left behind both in terms of available resources and policy-making. Especially during floods, the minimal access to resources prevents them from unclogging the drains and washing off the sludge, which is essential for reducing water levels. This leads to a vicious cycle for the *safai karamcharis*; their inability to clean worsens the flood levels, resulting in severe mobility issues in the community and leaving them to deal with the adverse effects of the calamity.

Amidst the exigent uncertainties, Basfores are forced to take up alternate tasks at their work and additional jobs on the side, to ensure a sufficient income stream. Often, they are asked to clean bathrooms or pick up additional garbage—roles not mentioned in their contract. Bi. Basfore commented,

> After the 2008 bomb blast in Guwahati, I was called to clean up the area including the roads and removal of dead bodies with the promise that my

Image 1 A safai karamchari works in a waste-filled drain in Colony 3 (Photograph by Rishiraj Sen)

job will be made permanent; but I was never offered a job. The same happened during Covid times, I was asked to clean the rooms and change diapers of the patients, they promised me a permanent job and money in exchange for the work but the job was not offered. Sometimes I look forward to the floods because at least I earn consistently then.

Even as other workplaces shut down under the emergency, none of the 32 respondents have had a day off amidst the life-threatening floods. Elaborating on the dire conditions, the respondents from Colony 3 Ar. and Su. Basfore stated that they would be *"replaced very easily if they don't go to work for even a day or refuse to do tasks apart from the contracted work. Our livelihood will be put to a stop."* Sundays mark their only "free" days, which they spend doing any and all odd jobs to not fall into a worse economic state. These appalling circumstances are echoed across roles in the sanitation workspace.

4.2 *Living Through Floods: Social Conditions of Safai Karamcharis*

Despite covering all bases, at the cost of overworking themselves, *safai karamcharis* are struggling to make ends meet. The average income in the sample was reported as Rs. 7,015.38, less than a third of the Guwahati city average salary of Rs. 25,833. This amount is insufficient to live in cities as the average cost of living in Guwahati was reported to be Rs. 16,042 for a family of two (Mehta, 2019). The average family size recorded in the sanitation worker sample was approximately five. The income earned by *safai karamcharis* will be insufficient to sustain a family of two, let alone an average of five. Adding to the pressure of irregular salaries and frequent health shocks during floods, this amount is grossly insufficient even for the most senior sanitation workers. Thus, they borrow money to fulfill daily necessary requirements such as food, water, and electricity.

The lack of access to BPL cards forces sanitation folks to purchase staples such as rice and pulses at market prices, even during floods. Drinking water is sold at Rs. 25/liter and is limited to 10 liters per household—the flood situation puts a stop to this entirely. The colony residents then depend on waste-filled drains for water. Electricity prices take up almost 1/3rd of their monthly income, amounting to a large sum (Rs. 1000–2000) of their undervalued salaries. Providing for the cost of essential goods on minimal to no savings poses unceasing challenges. Lack of reserve funds forces 78% of individuals to procure credit from formal and informal sources. This includes seeking loans from individuals/relatives (81.25%), banks (12.5%), and a combination of the two (6.25%). More often than not, *safai karamcharis* pays interest as high as 20%, which results in a debt trap. Minimal and unstable income streams prevent them from availing of low-interest loans from banks, even during the time of disasters.

In a related vein, unlike regular urban residents, sanitation workers bear additional costs on fixed assets, such as their homes. Owing to floods, roof leaks, and overflowing homes have been an annual occurrence over the past few decades. Yet, residents of the Harijan colonies have not been able to prepare for this due to deteriorating economic circumstances. This situation limits access to and from the colonies, trapping the residents to their locales.

> The drinking water trucks have not come to this colony for the past few days, everyone is dependent on the school well. There are 200 or so families here, some with very young children. If an emergency occurs due to the floods and the rains or if my children fall sick, no ambulance can reach here, no one will think of us. If not us, I want someone to at least think of my children. Su. Basfore from Colony 3 elaborated.

Their hard work, throughout the year and amidst these surges, does not reap any benefits. Even though sanitation workers clean up after everyone, they do not have any security net to fall back on. The circumstances of *safai karamcharis'* work, such as foul smells and its degrading nature, push them to consume alcohol. Unreliability of the quality of alcohol causes short-term illnesses, and prolonged intake leads to irreversible long-term effects (Rangamani et al., 2015; Sakthivel et al., 2019). The widows interviewed as a part of this ethnographic study also attributed their spouse's demise to habitual alcohol consumption.

4.3 Gender Polarities During Floods

Flooding has been an apparent struggle for the residents of Guwahati and has 'conveniently' become a part of their mundane life. While a disaster does not 'choose' who would be worst affected, the fragile socio-ecological systems, juxtaposed with social stratification, make some more vulnerable than others (Reid, 2013). The caste, class, and gender-based hierarchical system relegates 'others' to unequal access to protective measures. Building on Kimberlé Crenshaw's theory of intersectionality (1991), it is important to incorporate "an analytical sensibility" in thinking about identity and its relation to resource allocation. Women from lower caste backgrounds, in this case specifically, become more likely to face the ramifications of the rampant flooding (Image 2).

The ubiquitous inequalities that persist in Guwahati have left the female *safai karamcharis* at a significant disadvantage compared to the privileged folks in the city (Saad, 2021). Belonging to lower caste and class backgrounds, these women are forced to continue to work despite living through tumultuous floods. Some women report living with other family members in already cramped households. Regardless of the rising water levels and growing safety concerns, women are expected to travel through the waters on foot to fulfill their job requirements and earn money to sustain the household. Furthermore, women in the sample report experiencing acute discomfort while menstruating, yet having to undertake strenuous physical labor throughout the entire period. Bi.

Image 2 Women at the colony in Uzanbazar (Photograph by Rishiraj Sen)

Basfore, a forty-something sanitation worker, recounts sustaining an injury during work, yet not getting a day off. "*The only item I get from my employer is a badge with my name on it. Nothing else.*"

The Assam Government specifies the minimum wage for sanitation work to be Rs. 7200 per month; more than 50% of the sample earns less than the mandate (Office of Labour Commissioner, Assa, Government of Assam, 2022). The pressure especially increases manifolds on widows as they are the only viable income source to hold the family together. B. Basfore, an over-40-year-old widowed mother who has been working as a sanitation worker for a significant portion of her life, remarked,

> This is my mother's home. My house is completely flooded. Out of the seven days it rains, my own house is flooding for six. I find myself oscillating between the two houses. During floods, the challenges are numerous. I keep an umbrella on me, it's my only protection from these conditions.

More often than not, floods lead women to travel longer distances and undertake additional duties. From schools and government offices to household chores, the women in this sample have to diversify their income sources to earn around Rs. 3000 to Rs. 13,000 and support their families. This significant range of variable income is the factor of some women working at more than five locations on a daily basis to support the increased needs of their larger households. When widowed, she takes up the mantle as the breadwinner of the family—putting up a tough fight against all the odds stacked against her. To the degree of the flash floods, neither an illness nor a disaster excuses them from showing up to work.

While it is true that men working in the sanitation industry have to work additional shifts as well, women succumb to a "double burden" (Friedan, 1963). Adding to the long days of underpaid work, many women return to their homes promptly to attend to a plethora of household chores. This includes catering to the nutrition and health requirements of the family that are waiting to be fulfilled and replenishing clean water stocks that are often absent in these colonies. During rains and floods, the few water streams in their closer vicinity are muddied and rendered inaccessible.

In this situation, the women of the household travel long distances with buckets and pots balanced over their heads and in their hands to collect clean, sanitary water. The patriarchal notion of gender dichotomy ascribes women as "servers" who are required to cater to the needs of their family members (Beauvoir, 1974; Bhasin, 2006). Adding to her care and nurturing duties, she is also delegated the task of keeping flood water out of her home. In conjunction with their child-rearing responsibilities, all of the above roles leave little to no time for the women to rejuvenate themselves (Image 3).

The inability to meet the requisite role assignments has dire repercussions on women, especially during a disaster episode when the stressors multiply. Studies also show that women have a heightened tendency to experience gender-based and emotional violence during floods (Bradley et al., 2021; Nellemann et al., 2011). Among other socio-economic stressors associated with flooding, the increase in alcohol consumption exacerbates the occurrences of cases of abuse. While most incidents go unreported, studies have conclusively shown a positive correlation

Image 3 A woman from the Harijan Colony of Uzanbazar on her way to collect water (Photograph by Rishiraj Sen)

between disasters, intoxication, and gendered violence (Bradley et al., 2021).

In the case of male sanitation workers, where alcohol intake is a part of their daily diet, the intensity of violence increases significantly during trying times (Participatory Research in Asia, 2019). The field ethnographers noted a few women who went off the record to talk about their experience with violence from their spouses. The intrinsically connected socio-economic, political, and environmental aspects that are disturbed during a disaster expose the already vulnerable group(s) to more adversity than the rest.

5 Conclusion

A limitation of the aforementioned arguments lies in leaving out the effects of climate change and pollution, which sanitation workers both depend on and face the consequences of. While there exists an extensive literature on urban flooding and its relation to nature and waste generation, there is a dearth of a nuanced look at the people most vulnerable to it (Aravind, 2022; Jha et al., 2012; Lamond et al., 2012). Looking at this from an ethnographic perspective and after taking inspiration from Coulthard's wellness framework (2018), the intertwined links between the annual Assam floods and the overlooked work circumstances of *safai karamcharis* have been highlighted.

Employing a feminist methodology approach helped in nuancing the responses we were forced to collect in the limited time we were presented with. Being aware of our positionality while talking to not just safai karamcharis but also residents outside this community help us build a polyvocal narrative. Collaboration, across geographies and even between various respondents, helped in not forming a closed narrative around the community and every observation mentioned as a part of this chapter was what the respondents wished were widely known about them.

As the colony residents had continuously stated, visibility is lacking for this sector in all senses of the word. Disaster reports previously released on Assam floods by the state government, and other leading non-profit organizations, fail to include the plight of sanitation workers, much less acknowledge their role in maintaining the hygiene standards of Guwahati (Duncan et al., 2020; UNICEF, 2022). From a geographical perspective, the reports did not account for the four Harijan colonies studied or rather mention them as vulnerable locales.

Compared to crises of much larger scales, endemic conditions of the safai karamcharis do not seem to take priority enough to make visible changes. The loopholes in existing policies involving contracts and their "formality" fall flat in the face of the fragmented structure of the sector. Since the workforce is split into casual workers and those with a tiered seniority system, it becomes increasingly difficult to formulate welfare policies, especially in disaster situations. Even within the workforce, female *safai karamcharis* are paid much less for equally, if not more, strenuous work. Policy focus on widows, especially defined on the financial front, will provide security in the living conditions. Exclusionary flood relief policies barely reach these folks living in central yet neglected spaces of the city, as they are left to live with flooding kutcha houses and empty pockets.

References

Aravind, I. (2022, July 23). Why Urban Planners Need to Urgently Factor in Climate Change Mitigation. *The Economic Times*. https://economictimes.indiatimes.com/news/india/why-urban-planners-need-to-urgently-factor-in-climate-change-mitigation/articleshow/93078899.cms?from=mdr

Arksey, H., & Knight, P. (1999). *Interviewing for Social Scientists*. SAGE Publications, Ltd. https://doi.org/10.4135/9781849209335

Assam floods rehab: Centre to bear 90% of cost. (2022, July 17). *The Times of India*. https://timesofindia.indiatimes.com/india/assam-floods-rehab-centre-to-bear-90-of-cost/articleshow/92928359.cms

Basole, A. (2014, October). The Informal Sector from a Knowledge Perspective. *Down to Earth*, *Yojana* (Loka-Vidya), pp. 8–13.

Beauvoir, S. de. (1974). *The Second Sex* (H. M. Parshley, Trans.; First Vintage Books ed.). Vintage Books.

Bharathi, N., Malghan, D. V., & Rahman, A. (2018). *Isolated by Caste: Neighbourhood-Scale Residential Segregation in Indian Metros* (SSRN Scholarly Paper 3195672). https://doi.org/10.2139/ssrn.3195672

Bhasin, K. (2006). *What Is Patriarchy*. Women Limited.

Bradley, T., Martin, Z., Upreti, B. R., Subedu, B., & Shrestha, S. (2021). Gender and Disaster: The Impact of Natural Disasters on Violence Against Women in Nepal. *Journal of Asian and African Studies*, 002190962110624. https://doi.org/10.1177/00219096211062474

Coulthard, S., Mcgregor, J. A., & White, C. S. (2018). Chapter 15: Multiple Dimensions of Wellbeing in Practice. In K. Schreckenberg, G. Mace, & M. Poudyal (Eds.), *Ecosystem Services and Poverty Alleviation: Trade-offs and Governance* (pp. 243–256). Routledge.

Crenshaw, K. (1991). Mapping the Margins: Intersectionality, Identity Politics, and Violence against Women of Color. *Stanford Law Review, 43*(6), 1241. https://doi.org/10.2307/1229039

Duncan, A., Singh, G., & Jalf, I. (2020). *Assam-India Flood 2019 Final Report.* Water Survival Box and Khalsa Aid International. https://watersurvivalbox.ch/wp-content/uploads/2021/01/Assam-Final-Report.v3.pdf

Friedan, B. (1963). *The Feminine Mystique.* Norton.

Gammarano, R., & Kapsos, S. (2018). *Decent Work and the Sustainable Development Goals: A Guidebook on SDG Labour Market Indicators.* International Labour Organization.

Harriss-White, B. (2017). Formality and Informality in an Indian Urban Waste Economy. *International Journal of Sociology and Social Policy, 37*(7/8), 417–434. https://doi.org/10.1108/IJSSP-07-2016-0084

Jha, A. K., Bloch, R., & Lamond, J. (2012b). *Cities and Flooding: A Guide to Integrated Urban Flood Risk Management for the 21st Century.* The World Bank. https://doi.org/10.1596/978-0-8213-8866-2

Jodkha, S. (2015). *Caste in Contemporary India.* Routledge.

Lamond, J., Bhattacharya, N., & Bloch, R. (2012). The Role of Solid Waste Management as a Response to Urban Flood Risk in Developing Countries, a Case Study Analysis. *WIT Transactions on Ecology and the Environment, 159*, 193–204. https://doi.org/10.2495/FRIAR120161

Lived Realities of Women Sanitation Workers in India (Engaged Citizens, Responsive City (ECRC)). (2019). Participatory Research in Asia. https://www.pria.org/knowledge_resource/1571820425_Lived_Realities_of_Women_Sanitation_Workers_in_India_20-10-19.pdf

Mehta, R. (2019, October 29). Want to Shift from Metro City? Here are Costs, Ease of Living Features of Tier 2 Towns. *The Economic Times.* https://economictimes.indiatimes.com/wealth/plan/want-to-shift-from-metro-city-here-are-costs-ease-of-living-features-of-tier-2-towns/articleshow/71771909.cms

Mohanty, A., & Wadhawan, S. (2021). *Mapping India's Climate Vulnerability: A District Level Assessment.* Council on Energy, Environment and Water (CEEW). https://www.ceew.in/sites/default/files/ceew-study-on-climate-change-vulnerability-index-and-district-level-risk-assessment.pdf

National Commission for Safai Karamcharis Act, 1993, 64 199364. (1994). https://legislative.gov.in/sites/default/files/A1993-64_0.pdf

Nellemann, C., Verma, R., & Hislop, L. (Eds.). (2011). *Women at the Frontline of Climate Change: Gender Risks and Hopes: A Rapid Response Assessment. United Nations Environment Programme, GRID-Arendal.* UNEP.

Rangamani, S., Obalesha, K. B., & Gaitonde, R. (2015). Health Issues of Sanitation Workers in a Town in Karnataka: Findings from a Lay Health-Monitoring Study. *The National Medical Journal of India, 28*(2), 70–73.

Reid, M. (2013). Disasters and Social Inequalities: Disasters and Social Inequalities. *Sociology Compass, 7*(11), 984–997. https://doi.org/10.1111/soc4.12080

Revised VDA (Minimum Wages) for Domestic Workers, Office of Labour Commissioner, Assam, Government of Assam. (2022). https://labourcommissioner.assam.gov.in/sites/default/files/swf_utility_folder/departments/coi_labour_uneecopscloud_com_oid_14/menu/document/revised_vda_minimum_wages_for_domestic_workers.pdf

Saad, R. (2021). Women and DRR in Urban Slums—Building Resilience Through Development. *International Journal of Disaster Risk Reduction, 60*, 102264. https://doi.org/10.1016/j.ijdrr.2021.102264

Sahgal, N., Evans, J., Salazar, A. M., Starr, K. J., & Corichi, M. (2021, June 29). Religion in India: Tolerance and Segregation. *Pew Research Center's Religion & Public Life Project*. https://www.pewresearch.org/religion/2021/06/29/religion-in-india-tolerance-and-segregation/

Sakthivel, P., Nirmalkumar, M., & Benjamin, A. (2019). Rights of Sanitation Workers in India. In P. Sakthivel, M. Nirmalkumar, & A. Benjamin (Eds.), *The Right to Sanitation in India* (pp. 346–379). Oxford University Press. https://doi.org/10.1093/oso/9780199489855.003.0013

Sankaran, S., Sekerdej, M., & von Hecker, U. (2017). The Role of Indian Caste Identity and Caste Inconsistent Norms on Status Representation. *Frontiers in Psychology, 8*.https://doi.org/10.3389/fpsyg.2017.00487

Sheikh, R. A., & Gaurav, S. (2020). Informal Work in India: A Tale of Two Definitions. *The European Journal of Development Research, 32*(4), 1105–1127. https://doi.org/10.1057/s41287-020-00258-z

Singh, E. (2016). *Caste System in India—A Historical Perspective*. Kalpaz Publications.

Singh, G., Vithayathil, T., & Pradhan, K. C. (2019). Recasting Inequality: Residential Segregation by Caste over Time in Urban India. *Environment and Urbanization, 31*(2), 615–634. https://doi.org/10.1177/0956247818812330

Smithson, J. (2000). Using and analysing focus groups: Limitations and possibilities. *International Journal of Social Research Methodology, 3*(2), 103–119. https://doi.org/10.1080/136455700405172

UNICEF India Humanitarian Situation Report (Assam, Floods). (2022). UNICEF. https://reliefweb.int/report/india/unicef-india-humanitarian-situation-report-assam-floods-27-june-2022

CHAPTER 5

Living Among Waste: Bachaikaris of Bhalswa

Shubhangi Derhgawen, Ashika Thomas, Deepanshu Mohan, and Jignesh Mistry

Abstract This chapter is a feminist ethnographic inquiry into an often-overlooked community of waste pickers, dwelling on the fringes of urban existence within the Bhalswa region of Delhi, India. Also known as *Bachaikaris*, these resilient individuals migrated from West Bengal and are instrumental in managing the legacy waste amassed at the landfill. This study endeavours to amplify the voices of waste pickers and expose the gendered dimensions of their struggles for recognition and dignity.

S. Derhgawen (✉) · A. Thomas · D. Mohan · J. Mistry
Centre for New Economics Studies, Jindal School of Liberal Arts and Humanities, O.P. Jindal Global University, Sonipat, India
e-mail: derhgawen.shubhangi@gmail.com

D. Mohan
e-mail: dmohan@jgu.edu.in

S. Derhgawen
Centre for Modern Indian Studies, Georg-August-Universität, Göttingen, Germany

A. Thomas
London School of Economics and Political Science, London, England

D. Mohan et al. (eds.), *Pan-India Stories of Informal Workers During Covid-19 Pandemic*, https://doi.org/10.1007/978-981-97-1525-1_5

Discrimination and marginalisation endure as these labourers bear the burden of societal perceptions that assign them to the lowest rungs of the caste hierarchy. At the heart of this investigation lies the intricate interplay of caste dynamics, gender inequities, and the involvement of children in this sector. In the Bhalswa vicinity, waste pickers additionally confront an array of challenges relating to labour conditions, citizenship, and the profound consequences of the COVID-19 pandemic. Therefore, the underlying theme is to foster a more equitable and inclusive approach to waste management.

Keywords Waste pickers · Migration · Feminist ethnography · Bhalswa · Caste · Gender polarity

1 Introduction

"It's okay if you want to write about us, but can you ensure that they (state) don't take away our right to work?" Sitting on a tattered mat, Babita Behra, a waste picker, gazed at us with a sense of despair. Her query demonstrated her determination to fight, though her countenance suggested that she had already lost hope. Looking at her daughter-in-law while shaking her head, she repeatedly uttered, "Khatta bondho korbe (they will shut the landfill)." This occurrence aptly exemplified the predicament of waste pickers across India. Stuck on the fringe of the city, far from mainstream society, thousands of waste pickers like Babita Behra feel like spectres; their presence is unrecognised, unseen, and disregarded. Their daily duties consist of managing all that the city has discarded for miles, removed from view, and hidden from the urban aesthetic.

The terms trash, garbage, and waste are all used to illustrate how we deal with refuse. It is described as "mobile and mutating," meaning it can't be easily classified and is constantly appearing in different places, making it difficult to contain and categorise (Bhaviskar & Gidwani, 2019). Given the heightened awareness of environmental issues in recent times, waste management has become an increasingly important topic worldwide. This involves transitioning from stationary objects to recycled and treated materials that can once again become useful to society. Within cities, waste management has important differences, one of which is legacy waste. A major challenge in India, legacy waste refers to that which has been collected and stored in a landfill for many years. The National Green Tribunal has reported that 3159 legacy waste dumpsites in the country have covered over 10,000 hectares of usable urban land (Yadav, 2022). The city of Delhi alone has three large landfills on its outskirts. Occupying 78.5 acres of land, the Bhalswa landfill stands at a staggering 62 metres height towards the northwest of the national capital (Image 1).

Across different cultures, waste and its management are often considered unclean, leading to the development of stereotypes about lower social classes and castes. The low-income migrant communities, who fall into this category, usually occupy landfills like Bhalswa, situated on the outskirts of urban environments. With limited housing options and work opportunities in other parts of the city, they settle in these areas, which are the city's garbage dumping and treatment sites (Jeelani & Sharma, 2019). This community of waste pickers mainly consists of different groups of migrants from West Bengal who practise Islam. On average, these individuals have been living in Delhi for 20 years. Our conversations revealed

Image 1 Waste-contaminated water gathered at the back of the Bhalswa landfill (Photography by Jignesh Mistry)

that the interactions between these groups are influenced by their regional identities and occupations.

Rooted in caste dynamics, the community's association with waste is deeply entrenched in racial and ethnic differences, which are said to be "marked on their bodies" (Bhaviskar & Gidwani, 2019). The excess waste at the Bhalswa landfill provided migrant communities with an opportunity to earn a livelihood by collecting, segregating, and selling waste. However, they endured challenging working conditions and faced extensive humiliation and discrimination from the rest of the population (Bhaviskar & Gidwani, 2019). Even amidst the ongoing environmental crisis, the contributions and struggles of waste collectors remain overlooked, and their proximity to waste is normalised (Gidwani, 2015). This chapter aims to document the lives of waste pickers and the ever-increasing need for their services due to the vast amounts of waste generation in India, underlined by a pandemic looming over the world.

2 Methodology

We recall the initial surprise upon first encountering Bhalswa landfill, visible from the highway to anyone entering or leaving Delhi. Even from a distance we could spot the makeshift structures and people working amidst the trash mountain. During our field research, we visited Tandoor Wali Gali and Rajiv Nagar, the primary locations near the landfill where most of these workers reside. They live in slum-like settlements that spread within a 500-metre radius of the main mound. We noticed that the area is dotted with temporary homes made from scraps such as tarpaulin and thermocol. Some families even built dilapidated huts directly on the grounds of the landfill. With minimal distinction between the wasteland and the residential area, discharge and wastewater often seep into these homes.

The dwellings are standard *jhuggi-jhopris* consisting of two rooms and a small fireplace for cooking, typically shared by four or five occupants, including the respondents, their partners, a few children, and sometimes elderly relatives. Any additional areas, including storage rooms, front yards, or terrace areas, are collectively used for segregated waste storage. Given the toxicity of the waste, the landfill is susceptible to frequent fires, leading many waste pickers to seek relocation away from the area. On the first day, we were invited into a house located at a distance of only 10–20 metres from the huge heap of waste. The dwelling had an improvised entrance and a unique bed-like structure made of thermocol. The room had a dry toilet covered by a sheet of cardboard, and every other area of the house was utilized to store the segregated waste. They had no room for washing and would often make a partition with some cloth outside their home and bathe there (Image 2).

The team's familiarity with the space a few years prior to the pandemic led us to revisit it this time around. Despite having migrated decades earlier, most conversations with the respondents took place in Bengali. To mitigate the language barrier, Mr. Sheikh Akbar Ali, a waste picker from the community and our primary contact on the field, became our translator. We interviewed 16 waste pickers and their relatives over a period of ten days. Despite the pandemic restrictions, around four preliminary visits were made to each neighbourhood. Although we were from the area and familiar with the general norms, there was a clear sense of distance between us and the respondents that we had to overcome.

Image 2 No clear distinction exists between the landfill site and the residences of the waste workers (Photograph by Jignesh Mistry)

A comprehensive questionnaire was developed based on these preliminary visits and the previous knowledge we had of the community and waste-picking profession. The development of the questionnaire was coordinated with the project team based at a local university not far from Bhalswa. After the first visit, we revised the questionnaire to include aspects of the waste pickers' relationship with the state and changes in the labour regime. We conducted semi-structured interviews during the preliminary recce, leading the respondents to go on tangents and hone in on the issues they considered to be imminent (Arksey & Knight, 1999). We interviewed two groups of waste pickers:

a. Independent waste pickers who scavenged the garbage and segregated it into bags, which were later sold to small contractors and businessmen at the end of every month, and
b. Daily wage workers who were employed by private companies to segregate the disposal collected from nearby housing societies.

Most respondents were uncomfortable with video interviews, so we relied mainly on the audio medium. This allowed respondents to protect their identity and share their thoughts freely. In most cases, respondents delved into their personal histories and experiences with waste which is both part of their work and domestic life, with each interview sometimes lasting around 30 to 45 minutes.

Typically, individuals close their noses with their hands or a handkerchief while passing by, in an effort to avoid the foul odour that emanates from the landfill. Consequently, as we walked through Tandoor Wali Gali, we could feel the unease among the locals. They do not expect people from outside the community to visit the area because they are aware of the general aversion to the foul smell. At the outset of our fieldwork, the majority of waste collectors would subtly assess if we are also repulsed by being close to waste. However, their judgement was not just around our repulsion with waste but also their identities, often tied to their caste status.

Caste politics is firmly embedded in the waste ecosystem, with those from the lower castes assigned the "dirtiest" work (Bhaviskar & Gidwani, 2019). Simply seeing a lower caste individual or their presence in sacred spaces such as temples or kitchens is deemed to contaminate everything with impurity. Unfortunately, some individuals continue to defend this as a matter of "hygiene." Since lower castes work in close proximity to waste, they are often considered "dirty" and "unhygienic." However, such claims reflect a dichotomy between upper and lower castes, perpetuated by the notion that the nature of their work renders lower castes "impure" from birth (Vij, 2014). The caste system dictates the kind of work each *varna* is "supposed" to do, which is passed on through generations by the "accident of birth." Consequently, waste pickers carry the identity and association of waste with them, on their bodies. It is a lens through which they perceive everything around them. Unfortunately, this created a huge division between "us" and "them" in our fieldwork process.

Such caste dynamics were widely visible in the area as most people from other societies did not give houses on rent to the members of the waste-picking community. In one of our conversations, we remember a construction worker mentioned that even if they have no work, they will never work at the landfill. "*This is not what our people do. This is for the dirty Bengali folk.*" This reaffirmed the hesitant glances and stoic faces of the waste pickers as we navigated the field site. We had to put concerted efforts to make it clear that we were not bothered by them or their profession. We invested time to understand their stories and experiences of casteist oppression. Since we also visited the area regularly for around 10 days, the waste collectors gradually started to welcome our presence. This resulted in them becoming more open with us with fewer inhibitions, even allowing us to speak to them inside their homes, which, more often than not, they deny access to.

Although we were not strangers to the place, our position in relation to the respondents continually oscillated between being welcomed and being scared of. Being an outsider, any signs or items which mark foreigners often led to hostility from the waste pickers. We noted that each time we conducted an interview, they closely watched our mobile phones, tripod, camera, and lapel microphone as symbols of distinction. We remember that when we first started talking and getting to know the respondents, they were more on guard. They would often ask for our names and details about our native villages to gauge if we belonged to upper or lower caste backgrounds. While they often expressed appreciation that we were there to talk to them and that the interactions with us felt like a conversation set on equal grounds, the moment we started the official interview with the equipment, the respondents would suddenly become more reclusive. The unfamiliarity with the equipment and also the notion of all these gadgets as a luxury, when they are scrambling for the bare minimum, was reflected in their attitude. In this way, we would often spend at least the first ten minutes of the interview trying to reassure the interviewee and would ask them to tell us a lot of stories to get the conversation on track.

To ensure a polyvocal narrative, we interviewed not just an equal number of men and women but also youth who were taking part in the waste picking and segregation work by aiding their mothers. We engaged in multiple discussions with them, alongside their parents. Since they were minors, we were unable to conduct formal interviews. Nevertheless, we acknowledged them as equal contributors to the (informal) workforce, just like their parents, and took their opinion off-the record. This ensured that our observations contained multiple voices, in turn making it an active collaboration among several stakeholders in the waste management system. To tie the threads together, we communicated with a private contractor who had hired a group of waste pickers we had previously interacted with. We were accompanied by a male acquaintance and encountered an instance of sexism by the respondent. During this interaction, we observed that despite our role as the ethnographers, asking questions about the study and sharing insights on our work, he solely directed his responses towards our male friends. The contractor even went as far as to avoid making eye contact with the female researchers from this group, essentially rendering them invisible within the conversation. This incident raised our consciousness about the varied dynamics of the area and heightened our attentiveness to the body language of interviewees (Images 3 and 4).

Interviewing stakeholders at various levels, made us familiar with power dynamics present which led to resistances to reveal information. During one interaction, where a family comprising two women declined to engage with us due to apprehensions that vocalising their concerns could garner unwarranted attention from officials, potentially endangering their source of income. This illustrates the dilemma faced by waste pickers in Bhalswa as they lack the power and a political platform to assert their position in society, despite being involved in a widespread occupation. It required significant effort on our part to persuade the workers in moments of resistance that the work we were undertaking was imperative. When we mentioned that we wanted to convey their experiences and concerns to influence policymakers to take action, it encouraged them. *"You are coming and asking questions, so we are answering. If someone else*

Image 3 Youth engaged in collecting segregated waste at the base of the Bhalswa landfill (Photograph by Jignesh Mistry)

asks questions, and we give information, then only we can let others know that we need access to these government policies. We need the government to recognise us and regulate our work. If no one comes here and asks us questions, then what do we do and where do we go?" Sheikh, a resident of Bhalswa, commented on the last day of the field study.

3 Observations: Life Among Waste

3.1 *Nature of Work*

The workday of autonomous waste pickers in Bhalswa starts as early as 6 a.m., and ends in the afternoon at around 2 p.m. When they come back with heaps of gathered waste, the family members assemble to sort the collected waste, separating items such as cardboard pieces, plastic bottles, and polythene bags into different piles. The waste pickers who are privately employed work in shifts for a fixed number of hours, typically ranging from 8 to 12 hours. Their entire day is occupied by working

Image 4 Children amidst sacks of waste (Photograph by Jignesh Mistry)

for these companies, and they do not receive any time off. Independent waste pickers, on the other hand, typically have working relationships with contractors who are members of the same community and have gradually grown their business over time. Therefore, workers have a paternal connection with their contractors and depend on them to mitigate their grievances.

Regrettably, waste pickers who are privately employed do not share the same bond. They commented that the job alleviates the unease of unstable wages and mostly enables them to earn a fixed monthly amount. Nonetheless, their employers show no concern for their well-being. "*If I ever find myself in trouble, I will only approach the former contractor. It could even be at 1 AM, but I am aware that he will always be there to help.*" "*He will assist me, but the private organisation I am employed by shows no concern towards me. They will replace me at their discretion,*" Muzamil Rahman, a waste collector contracted by a private company, explained. Since there is no formal institution representing the interests of waste pickers, such as a recognised workers' union, those who collect waste face obstacles in negotiating for higher wages or the reliable payment of minimum wages. This gap is manipulated by private companies that employ these workers without any established agreements. The lack of government support for workers and the failure to implement vocational or income-based safety nets lead to exploitation.

In regard to payment, the autonomous waste collectors revealed that the market is highly variable. They earn a favourable rate of approximately 20–22 rupees per kilogram of segregated plastic during the summer but during the rainy season and disruptive periods, such as the pandemic, their rate dropped to around 8 rupees per kilogram. The waste collectors disclosed that they sometimes succeed in negotiating these rates with the contractors. Even in 2022, the pandemic caused waste material rates to drop, leading workers to sell more to break even. Workers employed by private companies shared concerns about inconsistent and late payments, sometimes delayed by four months. They face difficulties in paying rent and purchasing basic needs such as water and electricity during these challenging times.

A simple way to assess a group's economic well-being is by examining their ability to obtain essential goods such as clean water, electricity, and food. During our ethnographic study and interviews, we noticed that waste pickers usually buy bottled drinking water from private vendors and rely on contaminated ground and surface water for other purposes. Nizam (52) revealed that this part of their monthly spending was significantly high. Workers spend up to 10,000 rupees a month on rent, food, water, and electricity. With a salary of only 12,000–15,000 rupees, they can barely afford to spend on education or save for the future. "*This work breaks my heart and soul, but I can't stop. I barely earn 15,000 to 16,000 a month, of which 3000 goes toward rent. It's really sad that I have to buy things like water on top of that. The government doesn't supply water or ration. I pay for everything and have no money left by the end of the month*," Mahmud commented.

3.2 *Migration and Sense of Citizenship*

Metropolitan city capitals such as Delhi have a migratory pull effect on rural populations. Large numbers of people abandon their agricultural practices, close down their small businesses, and embark on a challenging journey to the centres of economic growth in the hope of earning enough money to support themselves. The Bengali community residing in the

Bhalswa region of North Delhi migrated from parts of West Bengal due to a similar pull effect. The community back home thrived as the Bhalswa residents brought their families out of dire conditions. Currently, the majority of trade conducted by the waste-picking workers in both the Bhalswa and Ghazipur landfills of Delhi is conducted by the Bengali community. "*I departed from Bengal and initially relocated to Orissa before arriving in Delhi. Working under a contractor, I was engaged in tasks such as masonry and cement mixing…The contractor was exploitative and did not pay me, so I left that job and relocated to Delhi with my family,*" stated Ahmed Sheikh.

The prospect of improved pay has resulted in the separation of numerous families. Amal, a 40-year-old who has resided here for the past decade, faces challenging financial decisions to visit his family. "*My youngest two still live in my village, and their grandparents look after them. I last met them two years ago, but I haven't saved enough money to return home yet.*" During the pandemic, some workers opted to return to their villages, providing them with the opportunity to live with their children for a few months. However, this choice resulted in stagnant finances and a stop to household activities. As a result of a considerable influx of migrants and the consequent surplus of labour, individuals now confront the unsettling possibility of being easily replaceable. This situation adds to job insecurity in the already overcrowded waste-picking industry. The plentiful supply of labour present in an unorganised and informal workforce has also resulted in a gradual decrease in wages for waste workers over time.

Some workers confessed that living conditions in Delhi have been overwhelming as of late. They experience a feeling of neglect and isolation from the wider population, as they reside in the periphery. The majority lacks legal recognition without any access to documents such as Aadhaar cards, voter IDs, and ration cards. Others who possess these documents bear their native village addresses in the document, restricting their access to services. This prevents waste pickers from taking part in any elections in Delhi and, thus, being involved in the selection of their governing officials. Abdul, a first-generation resident of Bhalswa, expressed the challenges he faced in voting. Waste pickers typically travel to their home villages to cast their ballots during national and state elections, with transportation expenses sometimes reaching up to 10,000 rupees. Despite this, they remain dedicated to exercising their right to vote. Waste pickers within the sample, particularly women, share Abdul's feelings that acquiring the right to vote provides them with a sense of belonging and an emotional attachment to their "home," which has been largely missing since their relocation to Delhi. The workers possess a distorted comprehension of residentship, and their homesickness has left them feeling "stateless." The right to vote is the sole factor that endows them with recognition as citizens of the country. Mujamil Mir, another waste collector from Bhalswa, expressed, "*I spend money, take absence from work, and make efforts to vote since I fear that if I cease voting, my citizenship may be revoked. My name will be removed from the voter list.*"

3.3 Women and Waste Picking

While the role of the male waste pickers ends at mid-day, the female residents of these colonies face an additional burden. We observed that women who usually help their husbands segregate, bring sacks full of unsegregated waste to their houses and sort through the heaps in their living space; all while keeping an eye on their children and continuing with their household chores. "*Now it really doesn't matter whether I like this work or not. My only wish is to educate my children. I don't want my kids to step into this business of waste picking ever. My father did not care to educate me, hence I am here but I don't want the same for my kids,*" Mahira explained (Image 5).

We could not note any visibly stark gender segregation among the waste pickers. There was virtually no disparity in pay and the nature of work for both men and women was mostly similar. Nevertheless, women were encumbered with household responsibilities and had to juggle between work and family (which you will find is the case across the stories in the book). Although women bore this additional burden, we believe they maintained autonomy both in their jobs and their personal lives as they were well-versed in all aspects of household income and expenditure. Due to the double-shift work, women are often excluded from leisure in many parts of society. In certain nooks and crannies of the landfill area, women were frequently found relaxing and engaging with each other. Even if waste segregation occurs during the day, the women in our observed waste-picking community typically converse with their peers while working at a pace that suits them. Unlike the industrial workers in the area, these women exhibited a distinct sense of identity and freedom.

Although some respondents were adamant about not letting their children enter the waste industry, it was observed that mothers often take

Image 5 A Bengali waste picker family at Bhalswa (Photograph by Jignesh Mistry)

help from their children (especially their male children) in the task of waste segregation. Most parents here want their children to get educated, however, many of them had to drop out of school during the pandemic because they did not have access to mobile phones or laptops to attend online classes. "*My youngest child goes for waste-picking. I rely solely on him for money because I can't work by myself. He couldn't finish school because we couldn't afford a mobile,*" Shahana, a middle-aged waste picker told us.

3.4 *Changes After the Pandemic*

Scholar Nandini Sen conducted a comparable ethnographic investigation of waste pickers in the state of Bengal. Sen conveyed that numerous waste pickers chose to stay outside of the mainstream society and that it was this detachment from both the state and the society that enabled waste pickers to earn a livelihood from the city's discarded materials (Sen, 2018). Our study in Bhalswa yielded similar results. The management of waste generated by a city falls under the jurisdiction of the state, restricting access to these sites for workers. Nevertheless, waste pickers have carved out their own space beyond the state's formalities and mainstream society, rendering themselves invisible. By accessing dumping grounds and landfills, waste pickers have achieved a sense of autonomy and freedom in their informal work. The waste pickers gained independence through their ability to work flexible hours and have mostly enjoyed unlimited access to the landfill site. However, we found that things are a bit tumultuous.

In recent years, the waste management system in Delhi has undergone significant transformations. Due to increased neoliberal policies, private companies are now entrusted with the responsibility of waste management by the state government. As suggested by Sen, the dumping sites and landfills are state properties that have been accessed by waste pickers with minimal interference for a considerable time. In recent years, waste management in Delhi has been privatised, with dumping sites being auctioned off to private companies for control. As a result, the waste-picking community in Bhalswa is currently experiencing a transition where access to waste is no longer free or easy. In a time when the only type of resources available to these waste pickers is their labour, the state's neoliberal policies have caused the waste pickers to be dispossessed of their means of livelihood. Within this sector, the community is facing casualisation of labour as their only option is to work with the private companies that are gradually gaining dominance. In this environment, they are compelled to work for low wages, long hours, and without job security. As a result, the autonomy of the waste-picking community has been eroded, leading to a restructuring of their labour process, despite the fact that access to waste has been restricted.

On the field, we discovered a notable psychological predicament experienced by waste pickers. Despite expressing a strong dislike for their profession, these waste pickers are compelled to participate in it owing to the deficiency of alternative income prospects. The scarcity of viable employment choices in their home towns and their limited qualifications and social capital detract from their ability to obtain alternative work in the city. Ansari, a waste collector in Bhalswa, shared the challenges faced by many in his community when he said, "*This work is degrading, but I have no other choice and nowhere else to turn.*" Supporting their families financially and providing their children with an education leave them with no viable options.

Simultaneously with changes in the labour regime, a gradual erosion of waste pickers' resilience in pursuit of a better life has also been observed. The impact of COVID-19 and the escalating wave of privatisation have sown seeds of doubt, leading them to fear that their current fate is inescapable. This heightened fear of losing their sole source of income has driven them to tightly clutch onto their identity as waste pickers. They aim to remain concealed within the shadows of the city and to persist carrying out their work quietly in the fear of being noticed and evacuated.

4 Conclusion

Within the public service sector, a significant number of workers classified as either "unskilled" or "semi-skilled" have relocated from various parts of India, particularly the North and East, to engage in waste-picking activities in Delhi's National Capital Region. According to Sheikh, "*Since the pandemic outbreak, a notable increase in the influx of migrants seeking waste-picking work in Bhalswa has been observed. However, without support from the state, how will these workers be assimilated?*" This holds true for both disorganised and organised working environments. Following the COVID-19 pandemic, waste pickers have been greatly affected as there has been a decrease in their earnings, resulting in depleted savings. These individuals are now struggling to gain access to the landfill. During the recent Municipal Corporation elections in the country, the Delhi landfills became a major political topic. Responsibility for the country's weakened waste management was contested by the top-contending parties. The victorious Aam Aadmi Party announced its intention to decrease the buildup of legacy waste at designated sites and level the associated mounds. These are laudable steps towards improving how Delhi manages and treats solid waste. However, the political atmosphere of the region appears to be overlooking a key participant—the waste pickers—who play a crucial role in assisting the state in achieving its aims. Interwoven within caste and class dynamics, these workers depend solely on their labour for survival. The physical toll of their work is evident on their bodies, and with the rise of privatisation, their labour is all they have to offer to private corporations.

References

Arksey, H., & Knight, P. T. (1999). *Interviewing for Social Scientists*. SAGE Publications, Ltd. https://doi.org/10.4135/9781849209335

Bhaviskar, A., & Gidwani, V. (2019). The Lives of Waste and Pollution. *Economic & Political Weekly, 54*(47), 49–56.

Gidwani, V. (2015). The Work of Waste: Inside India's Infra-economy. *Transactions of the Institute of British Geographers, 40*(4), 575–595. https://doi.org/10.1111/tran.12094

Jeelani, G. & Sharma, M. (2019, August 18). Mr. PM, Delhi is Bursting at the Seams. *India Today*. https://www.indiatoday.in/mail-today/story/mr-pm-delhi-is-bursting-at-the-seams-1582138-2019-08-19

Sen, N. (2018). *Urban Marginalisation in South Asia: Waste Pickers in Calcutta*. Routledge. https://www.routledge.com/Urban-Marginalisation-in-South-Asia-Waste-Pickers-in-Calcutta/Sen/p/book/9780367589738

Vij, S. (2014, December 1). Between the Bathroom and the Kitchen, there is Caste [Text]. *Scroll.In*. http://scroll.in/article/692513/between-the-bathroom-and-the-kitchen-there-is-caste

Yadav, P. (2022, September 28). Explained: What Is Biomining and How Can It Solve The Problem of Waste. *India Times*. https://www.indiatimes.com/explainers/news/what-is-biomining-and-how-can-it-solve-the-problem-of-waste-580660.html

CHAPTER 6

Cycle of Poverty: Analysing the Social Structures of the Women of Kapashera

Hima Trisha Mohan, Ashika Thomas, Sakshi Chindaliya, and Jignesh Mistry

Abstract This feminist ethnographic study explores the intersection of work, informality, and gender dynamics in Kapashera, a peri-urban settlement on the outskirts of Delhi, focusing on rural–urban migrant workers. Methodologically, it employs in-depth interviews and participant observation to uncover the challenges faced by this community. Findings reveal blurred distinctions between permanent and contractual employment,

---

H. T. Mohan (✉) · J. Mistry
Centre for New Economics Studies, Jindal School of Liberal Arts and Humanities, O.P. Jindal Global University, Sonipat, India
e-mail: 19jgls-hima.tm@jgu.edu.in

J. Mistry
e-mail: jignesh1104@gmail.com

H. T. Mohan
Jindal Global Law School, Sonipat, India

A. Thomas
London School of Economics and Political Science, London, England
e-mail: ashikathms@gmail.com

D. Mohan et al. (eds.), *Pan-India Stories of Informal Workers During Covid-19 Pandemic*, https://doi.org/10.1007/978-981-97-1525-1_6

heightened exploitation post-COVID due to increased subcontracting, and gender-specific challenges for women in exploitative working conditions. The study underscores the urgent need for policy interventions addressing workers' rights, subcontracting issues, and gender disparities in the informal labour sector.

Keywords Migration · Kapashera · Feminist ethnography · Neo-bondage · Unionisation · Gender

1 Introduction

"*Madam, stray dogs live better lives than I ever will. Is this what you want to hear from us?,*" a migrant worker searching for home and belonging in the peri-urban fringes of Delhi exclaimed on our first visit to Kapashera. His reaction, marred with anxiety, pointed towards the fear of inequitable access to resources, an impending evacuation, and being stripped of his makeshift life. He had found himself at the crossroads of claiming his space far from home and remaining an "equal" citizen, trying to negotiate his identity and agency. In fact, this was not a solitary response. Several others, who migrated to Delhi with aspirations for economic stability, echoed this concern.

The geospatiality of urban slums in India is a matter of concern that has become a pressing issue since the advent of neoliberalism and the exponential urbanisation of the country. Over the past few decades, India has witnessed a remarkable shift in its population distribution, with the percentage of people residing in cities escalating significantly. From a mere 18% in 1950, this urban population has climbed to 32% in 2013, and projections suggest it will reach a staggering 55% by 2050 (Peppercorn, 2013). Urban areas are increasingly sought after as a haven from economic trepidation by members of all castes and classes, leading to "slum-like" areas expanding and becoming densely populated. These

S. Chindaliya
Jindal School of Liberal Arts and Humanities, O.P Jindal Global University, Sonipat, India
e-mail: sakshichindaliya@yahoo.in

regions become the destination for low-income rural–urban migrant workers, who often settle into makeshift dwellings with only basic amenities. The spaces occupied by these allegedly inferior migrant groups often become a blindspot for development projects, with the residents left to fend for themselves with scarce resources (Wilson, 1987).

While several people commute across the diverse locales of Delhi and the National Capital Region (NCR) daily, these migrant colonies are often overlooked as collateral damage to the city's gentrification projects. There is a myriad of migrant experiences and stories pincushioned in these neglected areas, and one such example is Kapashera. Therefore, as an attempt to explore and engage with the power geometries of the space, a team of ethnographers began exploring Kapashera in early 2021. Situated on the Delhi-Haryana border, this locality has become home to thousands of migrant workers, mainly hailing from Uttar Pradesh and Bihar. These are some of the most poverty-stricken states in India, with an unemployment rate of 12% and 4%, respectively (Somayya, 2023). Kapashera's spatiality mirrors Dey's (2018) analysis of the historical chawls in Mumbai, emphasising the geographical isolation and the subsequent challenges faced by urban slums. With origins rooted in the textile industry of Udyog Vihar, Haryana, Kapashera attracts a significant number of migrant workers, primarily engaged in stitching jobs.

Tucked away near the Delhi-Haryana border, Kapashera is inviziblised amidst the hustle-bustle of the interstate route. The slum settlements are alienated from convenient access to essential services, educational facilities, and employment opportunities, which are typically concentrated in central Delhi. At first glance, the settlement's spatial layout reflects the dire living conditions of its inhabitants, but the deep-rooted scarcity of resources was not well-hidden. Families, often comprising five members, were accommodated in small one-room apartments with the kitchen squeezed into a corner, equipped with a utilitarian stove and gas. Communal toilets and bathing areas were shared by all the residents of the building, resulting in inevitable hygiene concerns. The spatial setup of Kapashera exemplifies the subpar living standards of urban slum settlements.

The congested area housing thousands of residents has provided rural migrants a space to chase their economic aspirations. People who have set up homes in Kapashera have been employed as skilled and unskilled labourers in the budding industrial belts surrounding the neighbourhood. However, the residents of the place share a sense of financial insecurity as most of them are employed on a contractual or daily wage basis. In addition to that, there has been a substantial decline in job opportunities, which, in turn, has weakened community institutions and diminished strong social networks. Ultimately, this has been a multiplier factor in fuelling the vicious cycle of poverty and social isolation within Kapashera and other urban slum settlements (Wilson, 1987).

To make matters worse, the implementation of several unprecedented government policies and sudden changes in economic structures exposed workers in Kapashera to further distress. The unanticipated demonetisation enacted by the Government of India in 2016, and the subsequent adoption of Goods and Services Tax in 2017, had a profound impact on the lives and livelihoods of residents of the space. While the ones who were financially affluent and held power faced minimal repercussions of the discontinuation of the 500- and 1000-rupee denominations, the informal workers faced the brunt of it. The shortage of cash meant that the doors were shut on employment opportunities and savings for contractual and daily wage labourers. Not only that, but several workers also lost their jobs in the midst of business closures and downsizing (Sarkar, 2016). Similarly, the introduction of GST brought an increase in taxes and compliance requirements, making it challenging for small businesses to remain viable. Ultimately, numerous micro and mini clothing factories were shut, exacerbating the economic challenges faced by the residents and workers of Kapashera. The situation was further worsened by the outbreak of the pandemic when the already declining earnings and job opportunities reached an all-time low. Manish Kumar, a migrant worker, emphasised the negative effects of demonetisation, GST, and the pandemic, saying that the businesses had roughly 50% fewer employees (Ahmad, 2021).

In this context, an ethnographic study and survey were carried out in the bustling city to comprehend the nuances and lived experiences of the informal rural–urban migrant workers in Kapashera. We specifically looked at the role played by the pandemic in exacerbating class differences. The survey and interview questions, conducted first in early 2021 and next in February 2023, were designed to examine nuances of their socio-cultural realities, adjacent to the apparent financial problems faced by the residents. This chapter dives into the lives and livelihoods of low-income, semi-skilled rural–urban migrants, examining the urban environments in which they live, their role played by the pandemic in financial and health-related issues, the informal undertones of their seemingly formal jobs, and the glaring gender divide.

2 Methodology

This study employed a feminist ethnographic approach to explore the complex socio-economic dimensions of Kapashera. Our team of three field ethnographers, over a three-month period in early 2021 and a month in March 2023, spoke to 165 respondents. We conducted the interviews with the help of a group of young NGO workers at Ideal Youth for Revolutionary Changes (IYRC), an organisation dedicated to empowering second-generation migrant children within Kapashera through education. As a first step, we familiarised ourselves with the geography of the area, making note of every single observation we had as a group of researchers who were (partial if not full) outsiders. My first reconnaissance in Kapashera was a mixed experience. The group of locals from the NGO that guided me showed the conditions of workers in Kapashera: the tightly packed living spaces, children running around playing games, narrow streets that could barely fit in a rickshaw, and the chaos of the marketplace.

Before going into the field, we were aware of ethnographic research being a very powerful method for delving into the intricacies of human societies and cultures. While we knew it was a process that demanded not only rigorous engagement but also an open heart and mind, it was often very difficult to immerse ourselves into the community we were studying. As noted by Shubhangi, a co-researcher in this project, "*Whenever I'm doing any study, I try to map each and every aspect of the field. However, personally, these experiences can feel suffocating because, in a way, I come from a different space. Encountering such unfamiliar spaces can be disorienting; you realise that 'this is how it is' from their perspective. Their work, sold and exported without much credit, remains limited in recognition and knowledge. While I have strong opinions when reflecting on it, in the field, I must adhere to the switch-off and switch-on mode. Opinions must be set aside; otherwise, they cloud objectivity.*"

At the heart of this methodology was participant observation, a process through which our team, as ethnographers, drew observations by trying to immerse ourselves in Kapashera's social fabric. "*It involved not only watching but actively participating in the local events, rituals, and routines*," as Shubhangi emphasised. This approach, for us, was pivotal in breaking down barriers and opening doors to candid conversations, providing an authentic window into the lives of Kapashera's inhabitants. Our first step in this sense, was to develop a comprehensive questionnaire. This initial step was informed by our extensive visits to the neighbourhood and drawing from our first leg of interviews, which aimed to gain insights into their diverse socio-economic backgrounds and challenges. Our collaborative efforts in constructing the questionnaire involved close coordination between the project team in Kapashera, along with the insights of the team at IYRC.

The process of questionnaire development was marked by a thorough review of secondary literature on informality among migrant workers and insightful discussions following our preliminary reconnaissance. Our primary objective was to create a questionnaire that not only captured the community's socio-economic profiles but also delved into their unique vulnerabilities to both short-term and long-term factors, such as law, policy and the impact of the COVID-19 pandemic. While we aspired to design a holistic questionnaire, after a few rounds of testing, we realised that the questions necessitated frequent revisions. This adaptability was crucial as each worker within Kapashera faced a distinct set of household and work-related challenges. We documented issues ranging from chronic health conditions arising out-of-the-work environment to the gendered complexities of family life. To accommodate these variations, we adopted a semi-structured interview format. This approach allowed workers to express their specific circumstances in a personalised, first-person narrative.

Utilising feminist ethnographic methods, in a space largely consisting of cis-male rural–urban migrants, we understood ethnography as an approach that places a central focus on addressing social inequalities as they pertain to the lives of men, women, and children within the community. This approach, for us, broadened the scope of feminist ethnography, emphasising the importance of its flexible and inclusive definition. A significant portion of feminist anthropology has traditionally concentrated on women as its primary subjects—particularly the works of women anthropologists studying other women. In our analysis, we tried to adopt a more expansive conception of the relationship between feminist theories. Based on this conception, social movements suggest that women should not be viewed as the exclusive subjects, authors, or recipients of feminist ethnography (Visweswaran, 1997). This perspective encouraged us in the reading of various forms of critical ethnography as valuable contributions to the understanding of complex social dynamics within Kapashera.

Conducting fieldwork in Kapashera brought forth a distinctive array of challenges, with language barrier emerging as one of the most significant hurdles to navigate. As one of the authors is a South Indian woman, she lacked a strong command of the local language, which was largely regional dialects of Hindi, depending on the state from which the worker had migrated. This inevitably created communication gaps between us and the community members. The linguistic divide posed an obstacle to effective data collection and meaningful interactions. In the face of this challenge, the team at IYRC acted as interpreters in the research process. Their role transcended mere translation; they became essential conduits for bridging the linguistic chasm between our team of ethnographers and the local residents. They not only facilitated conversations but also played a pivotal role in ensuring the accuracy and nuance of the data collected.

However, it is important to note that while the IYRC team was instrumental in mitigating the language barrier, they added another dimension to the research process. We knew we had to be wary of the nuance that might be lost in translation, and so we had to factor in the dissonance in our data collection cycle. We also developed feedback circuits for cross-checking and verifying data meticulously. In addition to that, IYRC did not just aid us as linguistic intermediaries; they were often embedded within the community and brought their own perspectives and biases to the table. Navigating these complexities required a delicate balance between reliance on the team and maintaining a critical perspective.

The next challenge that arose was trying to strike a balance between maintaining objectivity and empathy while knowing that establishing an emotional connection is key to gaining deeper insights into the community's psyche. As Shubhangi notes,

> In Kapashera, they harbour no aspirations toward change. I would assert that grappling with this reality, an accepted status quo is one of the most challenging aspects of fieldwork. It can evoke a sense of helplessness that lingers for a brief hour or so. However, my extensive practice of compartmentalization enables me to move past it eventually. Nevertheless, I must acknowledge that this particular challenge remains the most formidable to overcome during fieldwork.

They have already lost hope. They don't possess it anymore. They're investing their time because they're thinking, 'Alright, it might benefit you.' I recall conversing with a labourer from Bihar; we were discussing the topic of voting and why she chose to vote. She expressed, 'I don't vote for myself because I understand it won't change my circumstances. My destiny seems sealed, and I can't alter it. I merely focus on survival, hoping not to falter. However, I participate in the voting process because I believe my vote can bring a glimmer of happiness to the person I vote for – it can make a difference in their life.'

It also became imperative to tread carefully and consciously avoid blurring the lines between researcher and activist roles. The ethical responsibility of maintaining objectivity was paramount. As a team, we understood that our mission was not to intervene in the lives of the community members actively but to listen, understand, and document their experiences. It was important for us to remember that we cannot get involved personally, underscoring our commitment to upholding the core tenets of ethnographic inquiry—to observe and comprehend without imposing external influence. This ethical stance was particularly significant given the nuanced challenges faced by the community. While we were privy to the hardships, inequalities, and vulnerabilities experienced by the low-income migrants, our primary duty was to serve as impartial observers. We recognised that becoming directly involved in addressing these issues could compromise the integrity of the research:

The biggest thing when it comes to being taken seriously in the field is establishing a connection with the people you're talking to. I remember, even after our initial field visit, which lasted for about 20 days, when we returned a few months later, they still recognized us. Even those who didn't directly engage in conversation with us would mention that someone told them about our research here. That makes a difference. However, there's a challenge in Kapashera, and it's related to the prevailing narrative around women. It's intrinsically centred on their domestic responsibilities, their children, husbands, marriages, and so on. Sometimes, while in the field, it's tempting to switch into a mode where we can provide information, empower, engage genuinely, and connect easily with them, Shubhangi added.

But, of course, we must resist that temptation because it would essentially make us activists. For instance, in Kapashera, when we observed IYRC's work, they actively engage with people, have conversations, and

> work towards creating change. It's a different approach. Many times, we felt a desire to do the same, but it's crucial to maintain a clear distinction. Our role as investigators and researchers is not to actively involve ourselves in solving their issues like activists would. This instinct to help and guide comes up in every study. People often express that they look to individuals like us, who are educated, as a glimmer of hope, hoping that things might change. They believe we can help them. However, we've learned to separate ourselves from this burden because it's easy to feel the pressure to get things done in the field. But the essence of research is that you can't expect immediate results. It's about understanding how people perceive the changes they're going through and whether they see them as problems or as areas where they need help.

In the first leg of the study, we saw that among Kapashera's broader socio-cultural issues, conservative gender dynamics significantly impacted data collection. The restricted visibility and agency of women posed a challenge as they were less accessible for interviews. *"Despite it being incredibly frustrating, this is an aspect that we really couldn't probe more into because there was immense resistance, especially from the male counterparts."* During the second leg of our ethnographic study, out of the 32 interviews conducted, 18 were married women working as daily wage workers and contracted employees in the textile export industry in Udyog Vihar. One of the key takeaways from our fieldwork was to look not at gender dynamics in isolation but at its intersection with issues like income, education, and health.

> Women's voices are often marginalised in Kapashera, but they have a lot to say about their experiences and challenges. Our role as ethnographers was to amplify those voices. The gender angle in our fieldwork revealed not just disparities but also opportunities for empowerment. It's a nuanced story that goes beyond stereotypes. We had to approach our interviews and observations with a sensitive gender lens. It was essential to understand the distinct experiences of men and women in this community. Unfortunately, gender norms in Kapashera are deeply entrenched, but there are also signs of change. Men and women in Kapashera have different coping strategies in the face of adversity. Understanding these gender-specific responses was a key aspect of our research.

One of the most prominent challenges that emerged was the restricted visibility and agency of women within the community. These constraints made it more challenging to access and engage with women for interviews and observations. The conservative norms and expectations surrounding women's roles within the household and society acted as a subtle yet powerful barrier. It limited their participation in public spaces and made them less accessible to interact with. The gendered division of labour often confined women to the domestic sphere, leaving them with limited opportunities for interaction beyond their immediate family circles. Understanding and respecting the community's gender-exclusive spaces and norms was crucial. These spaces often dictated where and how interactions could occur. For instance, certain areas might be considered off-limits for male researchers when women were present, and vice versa.

Overcoming these gender-related challenges demanded creative and adaptive strategies. We had to be patient and persistent, recognising that it might take longer to establish connections with female participants in the presence of their male partners. As female researchers, we were able to try to build trust and rapport with women in the community, and this helped bridge the gap and facilitate more candid conversations. We had to adjust our approach to ensure that the voices and experiences of women were not marginalised or overlooked. This meant allocating more time and resources to engage with women and adapt the research methodology to accommodate their schedules and comfort levels. In Kapashera, women's exclusion from public decision-making was a consequence of a gendered system shaped by capitalist development, serving as a poignant reminder of the peril of imposing misguided ideological categories onto the lives of others. Our experience speaking with working women supporting their entire family, also compelled us to confront the multifaceted nature of women's social positioning, leaving us with a dilemma—were they entirely independent or partially subordinate? (Leacock, 1978).

Overall, the fieldwork process in Kapashera required us to be cognisant of a multitude of the community's issues in order to build a holistic narrative that was not overly saturated.

3 Observations and Findings

3.1 Work and Informality in Kapashera

Kapashera has become a home to diverse identities swarming in close proximity. Most residents are people who have migrated from Uttar Pradesh and Bihar, in search of better job prospects to support their families. Hailing from rural spaces, they perceive the urbanised Delhi-NCR region as their chance for a better life. The reality, however, seldom matches their expectations. Despite being adjacent to rapid development projects, Kapashera can be marked as an informal space, wherein people from lower caste and class categories battle a shared uncertainty in social and economic conditions. Contributing to a large portion of the informal workforce, skilled and unskilled labourers are forced to seek out contractual or daily wage work, as permanent jobs are few and far between. However, it is not uncommon for labourers in Kapashera to refer to their jobs as permanent despite being hired on a contractual basis. Not only do they have a limited understanding of the legal and technical differences, but many workers also remain employed by the same company for extended periods of time, blurring the line between permanent and contractual employment.

In contrast to contractual employment, the daily wage system is even more precarious. Neither are these workers (typically) hired with a guarantee for work the next day nor are they entitled to any employee benefits. That being said, daily wage work is the most common kind of employment in Kapashera's textile and garment industries, owing to seasonal and market-dependent demand. In addition to that, casualisation is widespread in Kapashera, with many factories relying on temporary or contract workers (instead of permanent employees) to fill their labour needs. This comes as a result of companies seeking to reduce labour costs and increase flexibility. While these types of employment can provide a valuable source of income for workers, they come with significant drawbacks, including lower pay, limited job security, and fewer benefits. Job insecurity often looms over them, pushing them further down into precarity (Standing, 2011). Stuck in limbo, residents of this space are left with no choice but to compromise on their living conditions.

The complex interplay between the informalisation of labour and the dire living conditions that plague Kapashera corresponds to Jan Breman's (1999) conception of the "double freedom theory." According to this idea, the expansion of capitalism generally allows the working class to gain a double feeling of "freedom." The first is the liberation from relationships of servitude seen in traditional forms of feudal relationships. In rural areas, more often than not, there is an unspoken sense of expectation from the lower-caste and lower-class individuals to restrict themselves to a menial scope of jobs. The "urban dream" provides workers with a platform to migrate and claim their agency. The worker becomes free to move away from working for their feudal master, to whom they would be a "servant," and replace their sense of duty and social obligation with a relationship that is more contractual in nature. The second sense of freedom is the ability to get away from traditional means of production and to sell their labour on the open market for the highest possible wage. In reality, however, workers are simultaneously commodified and bonded, systematically held captive by a faux sense of choice.

Subsequently, in the capitalist economic structure, migrants in Kapashera find themselves stuck in neo-bondage, i.e. the "new" transactional relationship between bosses and workers, which is less personalised, of shorter duration, more contractual and is monetised (Breman, 2010). Numerous markers of neo-bondage are linked to this idea of "freedom" (or the lack thereof). These include, but are not limited to, the lack of clear contracts with just remuneration, appalling working conditions, and irregular wage payments. However, with doubts about the survival of themselves and their family looming over their heads, workers are left with no choice but to succumb to the substandard employment conditions. The employers, cognisant of the surplus of labour in the neo-liberal economy, often capitalise on these circumstances. From extending the day shift into the night and paying per piece of clothing stitched instead of time to involving workers' children and spouses with compensation, businesses were noted to be creating an exploitative work environment. Several respondents also commented upon the hostility at the workplace, marked by ignorance towards industrial hazards and unexplained docking of wages (Image 1).

Compelled by their circumstances, a significant proportion of the workforce in Kapashera works in tailoring, pressing, thread cutting, button making, and quality checking. Each of these clusters requires different skills and expertise. Tailors, at the top of the economic hierarchy, in this area, are responsible for stitching and assembling garments. They are skilled workers, with many of them having learnt the craft in their native villages or having started as helpers and worked their way up to the tailor level. Tailors are also paid better and have higher job security than workers in other clusters. Pressers, thread cutters, button makers, and quality checkers, on the other hand, are semi-skilled workers. Pressers are responsible for ironing and finishing garments, while thread cutters are responsible for finishing garments by removing lint or small excess threads. Button makers attach buttons to garments, while quality checkers ensure that the garments meet industry standards and specifications.

Image 1 Staff requirement posters and banners at Udyog Vihar, Kapashera Border, Gurugram (Photograph by Jignesh Mistry)

Prior to the pandemic, demand for each work cluster in Kapashera was high, with the garment export industry in India experiencing significant growth. However, the pandemic had a significant impact on the industry, with demand plummeting due to lockdowns and economic uncertainty. During the lockdown, many companies in Kapashera and other areas were forced to lay off workers due to a lack of demand and reduced production. Many workers, particularly women, returned to their native villages in search of work, while others remained in the area and struggled to find employment. As the situation improved and demand began to pick up, many workers returned to Kapashera and the nearby industrial area of Udyog Vihar to look for work. However, finding employment was not easy, and it often took workers about a month or longer to find new jobs. Moreover, many companies shut down after COVID-19 due to a loss in demand and capital, exacerbating the already challenging job market (Tripathi, 2020) (Image 2).

However, despite the challenges, many workers in Kapashera continued to largely work in the same roles as before the pandemic. This is due in

Image 2 Workers post-lockdown regulations at Udyog Vihar, Kapashera Border, Gurugram (Photograph by Jignesh Mistry)

part to the highly specialised nature of work in the area, as well as the lack of alternative employment opportunities for workers. Tailors, in particular, found work easily as they were skilled workers. However, labourers involved in finishing activities like thread cutting and pressing found it harder to get their jobs back as they were semi-skilled.

The work conditions in Kapashera are very harsh, with workers facing long hours, low wages, and poor working conditions. One of the key issues faced by workers is the importance of overtime earnings, which often make up a significant amount of their monthly savings. However, after the pandemic, there has been a diminishing amount of overtime available, which has impacted workers' earnings. The pandemic and the lockdown have had a severe impact on the economy, resulting in reduced demand for garments and textiles, which has had a significant impact on wages (Chourasiya et al. 2022) . However, we found that the respondents in Kapashera showed a similar pattern in the increase of wages for contractual labourers, particularly men, by 1000–2000 rupees.

During our field visits, it became evident that the workers in Kapashera lacked any awareness about their rights as employees. This was also associated with the pattern that in recent years, there has been a prevalence of increasing sub-contractual work in Kapashera. Companies outsource small tailoring jobs and other "finishing" jobs to fabricators, who then hire daily wage workers on a per-piece rate. This system has resulted in the exploitation of daily wage workers, who are often paid lower wages than contractual labourers.

In 2021, there was a slight improvement in work conditions in Kapashera, as a significant amount of backlog work from the previous pandemic year was addressed, leading to better pay. Nonetheless, the workers still grapple with the influence of the international political economy and the heightened participation of contractors in the fabricator system. These contractors often deduct a portion of the workers' wages, further reducing their earnings.

3.2 *Squeezing the Workforce*

As the involvement of contractors increased, an exploitative relationship developed between the workers and these contractors. In the contractual labour sector, workers noted that post-COVID, the per-piece rate for garments like shirts and pants increased. However, as highlighted earlier, due to the expanded subcontracting, a substantial portion of their earnings now goes to the contractors. Nilesh Tripathi, a tailor at a fabricator factory in Kapashera, explained, "*Before COVID, we earned Rs. 30 for a shirt; now, the rate is Rs. 50. Yet, we only receive Rs. 30 per piece because the middleman pockets Rs. 20 per piece*" (Image 3).

A parallel pattern was observed among daily wage workers, predominantly involving women in tasks like thread cutting and folding. These women recounted distressing experiences of exploitation. In contrast to pre-COVID conditions, women are now compelled to endure eight to twelve-hour standing shifts without breaks, resulting in adverse health effects. Regarding wages, women mentioned that pre-COVID, the daily wage was approximately 250 rupees. Post-COVID, it increased to 300 rupees for eight-hour shifts. Despite this raise, contractors continue to take their share, leaving workers with minimal or no real gains. The growing collaboration between contractors and companies has made it challenging for workers in both clusters to evade exploitation, as was possible before COVID when they were directly employed by companies.

Image 3 A garment stitching unit at Kapashera (Photograph by Shubhangi Derhgawen)

Rekha Devi, a daily wage worker, expressed, "*We often decline many jobs offered nowadays because of the requirement to stand throughout the work, causing significant pain in our limbs and joints.*"

Post-COVID, a majority of companies have shifted towards employing contractual or daily wage labour, resulting in heightened exploitation. The workers also noted increased pressure to meet target-oriented work requirements. Within their eight-hour shifts, they are assigned specific targets, and failure to achieve them leads to blacklisting. Rekha Devi emphasised, "*Now we are given hourly targets, and the quantity expectations are quite unreasonable. For instance, if we can realistically complete 60 garments in one hour, we are asked to do 120–130. If we fail to meet the target, they don't offer us work the following day.*"

The current workload in Udyog Vihar is disproportionately assigned to contractual labourers. Companies are extracting more work from these labourers while sidestepping extra pay by eliminating overtime opportunities. Daily wage worker Pintu Kumar highlighted changes in the work environment, stating, "*Contractors behave rudely, talk to us disrespectfully, and even confiscate our phones as soon as we start working.*" Grappling with the repercussions of the COVID-19 pandemic, migrant workers in Kapashera are witnessing a significant trend towards the casualisation of labour. Despite a diminishing demand for work, the pandemic has brought about substantial changes in working conditions. Capitalising on the vulnerability of workers, the export industry in Udyog Vihar has taken an unregulated exploitative turn.

3.3 Women in Kapashera

3.3.1 Exploitative Working Conditions

The industrial areas in and around Kapashera offer employment opportunities for migrant workers, but the working conditions are subpar and highly demanding, especially for women. The aftermath of the pandemic has worsened these conditions, leading to the exclusion of many women from the permanent labour force. Numerous women lost their jobs due to the pandemic, facing financial constraints that compelled them to return to their native villages despite challenging travel restrictions. In my interactions with Rekha Devi, she expressed her deep dissatisfaction with the situation as she and many others were laid off from permanent positions during the pandemic. Now relegated to daily wage work, they struggle to secure employment for more than 10 days a month. The available jobs for women are typically low-paying, requiring long hours, and leaving minimal time for rest or other activities. Out of the eighteen women we interviewed, only two were working in factories as part of the permanent labour force (Mitra and Sinha, 2021) (Image 4).

Comparatively, their husbands found jobs within 1 or 2 months on average after the lifting of the lockdown, while women found it much harder to find jobs, especially in the semi-skilled sector. Moreover, women often have to manage domestic responsibilities simultaneously, which takes a toll on their physical and mental health. Kiran Devi recalled, "*My husband and I worked in the same company pre-pandemic. He worked as a checker and I did stitching. However, we were laid off during the lockdown. My husband found work at another company relatively easily, whereas I am*

Image 4 Udyog Vihar Phase 2–3 at Gurugram, Kapashera Border (Photograph by Jignesh Mistry)

working as a daily wage worker since there is no demand and most companies are shutting down. I am hopeful that this will change after the Holi season."

The post-pandemic job market has been particularly challenging for women, as they are often seen as a liability by employers owing to their family responsibilities. Due to the lack of permanent job opportunities, many women in Kapashera have shifted to doing exploitative daily wage work, including finishing jobs such as thread cutting and button work. In this ecosystem, women are engaged in doing tasks that complete a garment for export. *Dhaaga cutting*, also known as thread cutting, is a tedious and repetitive job that requires workers to use scissors or other cutting tools to trim loose threads from garments. They get paid on a per-piece basis for these jobs, with contractors taking a large cut. These jobs pay very little and offer no job security, leaving women vulnerable to unfair treatment and poor working conditions. Susheela, 40, a daily wage worker who does hook and button stitching, said, "*I had to stand and work for 8–10 hours a day, and use to earn about Rs. 300 per day. Now, I can't do this kind of work anymore as my health has deteriorated. It is extremely tough for uneducated, semi-skilled women like me to find any jobs at all, forget well-paying ones.*"

Our findings demonstrated that the lack of job opportunities for women in Kapashera poses a significant challenge, as many of them are compelled to accept jobs that are physically demanding, low-paying, and require only basic skills. This arises from a number of institutional problems that impede women's ability to secure better-paying employment, including inadequate access to education and training that would enable them to enhance their skills. This situation not only negatively impacts migrant women, but also hinders the growth of the industrial area and, ultimately, the economy of the country.

3.3.2 Challenges to Unionisation

The women who were pushed out of the labour force, are forced to resort to daily wage work. They walk a few kilometres every morning and reach Udyog Vihar, the industrial area and wait for contractors to bring them work. This area, also known as the *Mazdoor Mandi*, is a crowded marketplace where women gather to find work in different factories. Many women expressed that they stand here from 8 a.m. to 12 p.m. hoping for work; otherwise, they are forced to head back home. Despite the large number of workers present, the issue of unionisation remains a major challenge for them (Image 5).

Examining the *Mazdoor Mandi* from a theoretical standpoint, it becomes a complex intersection of empowerment and exploitation for women. On one side of the spectrum, women workers, viewed through a feminist lens, find a source of empowerment. They establish a support network, forming a sisterhood that aids them in navigating challenging working conditions. Collaboratively, they negotiate for improved compensation per piece of finished cloth and share insights on avoiding physically demanding tasks. Conversely, the absence of unionisation and collective bargaining renders these women vulnerable to exploitation. Drawing on theories of labour economics, they become reliant on contractors who impose low wages and substandard working conditions. These contractors leverage the precarious living conditions of migrant women, coercing them into accepting reduced pay. Munni Devi, a daily wage worker at the Mandi, illustrates this dynamic, stating, "*We are entitled to earn 300 rupees for an eight-hour shift. However, contractors here offer 260rs for 10–12 hour shifts. While we advocate for increased wages, some vulnerable women give in to these demands as the day progresses, with*

Image 5 Daily wage women workers at "labour chowk," Udyog Vihar Phase-1, Gurugram (Photograph by Jignesh Mistry)

contractors easily taking a 40 rupee cut." This power imbalance leaves women in a precarious position, lacking the authority to negotiate for better terms.

In numerous instances, women find themselves in extremely challenging financial situations, intensifying the pressure to accept any available work, even if it entails labouring for extended hours with minimal compensation. Muniya Devi articulates this predicament, stating, "*We are afraid to take leaves even in difficult circumstances, as there is a fear of being laid off*." The absence of job security contributes to a constant apprehension about where the next paycheck will come from. Despite a shared understanding among workers about exploitation, a lack of collective bargaining or unionisation prevails. This absence of solidarity perpetuates a vicious cycle of exploitation. Capitalising on workers' vulnerabilities, contractors offer low wages, extended working hours, and substandard working conditions, as workers, driven by desperation, acquiesce to these terms. In the absence of collective bargaining, workers find themselves without the means to demand improved wages and working conditions, further reinforcing their powerlessness in the negotiation process.

3.3.3 Adverse Impact on the Health of Working Women

The exploitative working conditions in Kapashera have also resulted in a significant impact on the health of women workers. The majority of women who work in garment factories have nutrition-related health issues due to the strenuous nature of their work that demands them to stand and work for long hours continuously. As a result, workers suffer from conditions such as anaemia, high blood pressure, fatigue, and complaints of body pain. Further, we saw that low wages directly affect the nutritional intake of workers, as they cannot afford to buy nutritious food. This also plays out as a barrier to proper healthcare. Santosh, a tailor from Kapashera, said, "*I have low haemoglobin and require blood transfusion. Due to my low income, I am no longer getting the treatment done and am trying to cure it through my diet.*" This is often difficult as the residents have reported being malnourished with no means of accessing all the nutrients necessary, thus adding to their existing health conditions.

The lack of access to childcare facilities in Kapashera further compounds the challenges faced by women workers. Many women have young children but have no access to affordable childcare facilities. As a result, they struggle to balance the demands of work and childcare. This also impacts women's ability to work long hours, as they are unable to leave their children unattended for extended periods, having long-term implications for their income and career opportunities. Women who take time off to care for their children are often unable to return to the same level of employment or earn the same income as their male counterparts, perpetuating gender inequality in the labour force. Since the pandemic, the avenues for work have also reduced, leading to less flexibility in working hours. *Daily wage worker Kumari Kalpana said, "I am looking for a job that allows me to work at night. This way, I can take care of my kids during the day and go to work at night. But ever since the pandemic, all avenues of overtime work have shut down. So I am unable to find the kind of work I need."*

In addition to all this, we found that the burden of infertility falls completely on women. They are under immense pressure to conceive, and if they fail to do so, they are often blamed for it. This further adds to their stress, impacting their mental and physical health. Kumari Puja said,

"*I began working in order to pay for my fertility treatment as it has been six years since I got married and I do not have any kids yet. My salary of Rs. 10,000 used to be the amount I paid for the treatment I was getting.*" Once they do have children, they face additional responsibilities, which impacts their participation in the labour force. Many women who were pregnant during the course of the pandemic have since been pushed out of the labour force. These women also spoke about taking care of their in-laws and children, which adds to their already endless list of responsibilities. These additional burdens make it difficult for them to work according to the standards of efficiency desired by the exploitative industry.

3.3.4 Intra-household Bargaining Power

Women in Kapashera also face significant challenges when it comes to intra-household bargaining power. They have little to no say in decisions related to household consumption patterns, such as rent and ration, and when questioned, have no idea how much their husbands earn or what they do for a living. Munni Devi, a daily wage worker, said, "*My husband and son laugh at me if I ask them about such things.*"

This lack of information and participation in household decision-making limits women's ability to make decisions that heavily impact their lives and their families. Women are often financially dependent on their husbands and have little financial autonomy over their income. This lack of autonomy further exacerbates their vulnerability and limits their ability to make decisions related to their own health, education, and career opportunities. Only when women have avenues of work and are able to contribute to the household, can their financial autonomy be achieved. Many female respondents expressed that it was only when they started working that their salaries were managed and spent by them, with the husbands rarely having a say.

4 Conclusion

Kapashera embodies the struggles and aspirations of thousands of rural–urban migrant workers across the country. The story of this space reflects the broader narrative of marginalised communities grappling with the impact of urbanisation, economic policies, and global disruptions. The geospatial transformation brought about by rapid urbanisation and the influx of migrants from impoverished states has led to the formation of slum-like areas, where basic amenities and developmental projects remain elusive. Our ethnographic study, conducted with a feminist lens, delved into the lives of these migrant workers, particularly during the challenging times marked by demonetisation, the implementation of the Goods and Services Tax (GST), and the unprecedented disruptions caused by the COVID-19 pandemic. The economic uncertainties and job losses resulting from these events have exacerbated the vulnerabilities of the residents of Kapashera, leading to a vicious cycle of poverty and social isolation. The methodology we employed aimed to bridge the gap between researchers and the community.

The gender-specific challenges faced by women in Kapashera highlighted the deeply entrenched gender norms and the need for a nuanced understanding of their experiences. The restricted visibility and agency of women within the community posed obstacles to data collection, emphasising the importance of adapting research strategies to ensure their voices were not marginalised. The narratives shared by the community members shed light on their resilience, adaptability, and the urgent need for inclusive policies that address the multifaceted issues faced by those on the fringes of urban development. The findings of our study call for a holistic understanding of the challenges faced by migrant workers, urging policymakers and advocates to consider the interplay of the economic, social, and gender dynamics in crafting inclusive and sustainable solutions.

References

Ahmad, J. (2021). Impact of Demonetization and Goods and Services Tax (GST) on India's Economic Growth: A Critical Review. *South Asian Journal of Social Studies and Economics, 12*(4), 78–87. https://doi.org/10.9734/sajsse/2021/v12i430317

Breman, J. (1999). The Study of Industrial Labour in POST-colonial India—The Formal Sector: An Introductory Review. *Contributions to Indian Sociology, 33*(1–2), 1–41. https://doi.org/10.1177/006996679903300104

Breman, J. (2010). Neo-Bondage: A Fieldwork-Based Account. *International Labor and Working-Class History, 78*, 48–62.

Chourasiya, R., Pandey, S., & Malviya, R. K. (2022). Sustainable manufacturing adoption in textile industries: A systematic state-of-art literature review and future research outline. *Sustainable Development, 31*(2), 612–638. https://doi.org/10.1002/sd.2434

Dey, S. (2018). *The Circular Economy of Dharavi: Making Building Materials From Waste* [Master Thesis, PennState University]. https://etda.libraries.psu.edu/catalog/15724szd62

Leacock, E., et al. (1978). Women's Status in Egalitarian Society: Implications for Social Evolution. *Current Anthropology, 19*(2), 247–275. http://www.jstor.org/stable/2741993

Mitra, S., & Sinha, D. (2021). COVID-19 and Women's Labour Crisis: Reiterating an Inclusive Policy Response. *Review of Women's Studies, Economic & Political Weekly, 56*(17). https://www.epw.in/journal/2021/17/review-womens-studies/covid-19-and-womens-labour-crisis-reiterating.html

Peppercorn, I. (2013, October 21). *Beyond the City Limits: Report Finds Rapid Suburban Growth in India, Potential for Sustainable Cities to Reduce Poverty*. World Bank. https://doi.org/10/21/india-urbanization-report-beyond-sustainable-cities

Sarkar, A. (2016, December 5). Demonetisation Logic Not in Sync with Implementation Plan. *Deccan Herald*. https://www.deccanherald.com/opinion/demonetisation-logic-not-sync-implementation-2100385

Somayya K, N. (2023, May 1). *Unemployment rate heightened in April*. Centre for Monitoring Indian Economy Pvt. Ltd. https://www.cmie.com/kommon/bin/sr.php?kall=warticle&dt=20230501182648&msec=936

Standing, G. (2011). *The Precariat: The New Dangerous Class*. Bloomsbury Academic.https://doi.org/10.5040/9781849664554

Tripathi, B. (2020, May 13). *Relaxing Labour Laws Can't Help Industry In The Long Run; Formalising The Economy Can*. https://www.indiaspend.com/relaxing-labour-laws-cant-help-industry-in-the-long-run-formalising-the-economy-can/

Visweswaran, K. (1997). Histories of Feminist Ethnography. *Annual Review of Anthropology, 26*, 591–621. https://doi.org/10.1146/annurev.anthro.26.1.591

Wilson, W. J. (1987). *The Truly Disadvantaged: The Inner City, the Underclass, and Public Policy* (2nd ed.). University of Chicago Press.

World Employment and Social Outlook—Trends 2022. (n.d.). International Labour Organisation. Retrieved November 25, 2023, from https://www.ilo.org/global/research/global-reports/weso/trends2022/lang--en/index.htm

CHAPTER 7

Reflections

Ashika Thomas, Sakshi Chindaliya, Deepanshu Mohan, and Arun Kumar Kaushik

Abstract This chapter collates the findings observed when interacting with the multifaceted informal communities of India. Major trends were identified including gender disparities, youth participation in trades and income choices. From the fishing industry to sanitation work, the pandemic exposes and exacerbates existing hierarchies, with women

D. Mohan
Centre for New Economics Studies, O.P. Jindal School of Liberal Arts and Humanities, Jindal Global University, Sonipat, India
e-mail: dmohan@jgu.edu.in

A. Thomas (✉)
London School of Economics and Political Science, London, UK
e-mail: ashikathms@gmail.com

S. Chindaliya · D. Mohan · A. K. Kaushik
Jindal School of Liberal Arts and Humanities, O.P. Jindal Global University, Sonipat, India
e-mail: sakshichindaliya@yahoo.in

A. K. Kaushik
e-mail: akkaushik@jgu.edu.in

D. Mohan et al. (eds.), *Pan-India Stories of Informal Workers During Covid-19 Pandemic*, https://doi.org/10.1007/978-981-97-1525-1_7

bearing a "double burden" of domestic responsibilities and underpaid labor. The narrative extends to urban spaces, where women are relegated to informal sectors, facing mobility restrictions and wage disparities. Examining youth trends, the chapter observes a shift towards consumerism and technology-driven aspirations, especially in the post-80s neoliberal era. The narrative also delves into income choices, revealing how households, despite limited resources, invest in cultural capital through festivals. To bring the anthology to a full circle, the chapter reflects on feminist ethnographic methods, highlighting the intersection of activism and academic research. Based on interviews conducted with authors of case studies presented in the book it emphasizes the importance of navigating unpredictability, making research accessible, and fostering collaboration with communities. The insights underscore the ongoing dialogue between researchers and communities, challenging power structures, and advocating for social justice.

Keywords Feminist ethnography · Gender disparities · Informal spaces · Youth trends · Income choices · Activism in research · Community collaboration

1 I

Through this anthology, we discussed the lifestyles of the multifaceted communities of India, delving into the intricate narratives and lived experiences of dwellers of informal spaces from diverse walks of life. By means of visual storytelling, this book captured the pandemic for steel factories in the North to the unrelenting textile industries of the West, the flooded streets of Guwahati in the East to the coastal fishing hamlets in the South. The pandemic proved to be a varying experience not just based on one's income but the pre-crisis social status such as caste, geographic location, and livelihood. Hence, recording individual accounts and piecing them to form a larger community experience, we hope, will aid further research. We explore the broader implications of these narratives and their significance in the larger context of feminist scholarship and social change.

1.1 Gender

Within the realm of informal spaces in India, the profound impact of gender-differentiated exposure during the pandemic presented a complex web of challenges that women, especially those from marginalised backgrounds, navigate. Amidst the backdrop of the pandemic, the deeply entrenched socio-cultural and economic structures that have historically alienated women, placing them at a distinct disadvantage, became more apparent than ever. Hence, instead of approaching it from an equality perspective, we resorted to the lens of equity. This allowed us to analyse how women's diverse social identities intersect to produce specific and compounded consequences, shedding light on the "double burden" they bear (Friedan, 1963). Through our ethnography, we dove into the intricacies of their experiences, which provided insight into the often-invisibilised, overworked, and underpaid nature of their contributions to the economy.

For instance, contrary to the common perception of the fishing industry being primarily male-dominated, we found that women are central in the intricate supply chain of this unorganised sector. Despite engaging in all facets of the trade, except venturing out in the sea, their efforts are rarely accounted for in the mainstream discourse. The invisibilisation of their contributions not only reflects but also perpetuates the existing gender-based hierarchies. This gendered imbalance extends to other informal sectors as well, including sanitation work, where women face conditions that are less than favourable. During our fieldwork in Guwahati, we found that the inadequate wages and harsh working conditions in this industry exacerbated the disparities, with overworked and underpaid women carrying out essential work. The challenges were further heightened during floods, where women from lower caste and class backgrounds were disproportionately affected. Having to navigate through the murky waters, women were forced to continue their physically demanding work, even while menstruating.

In stark contrast, we observed how entrenched gender-based hierarchies and prescribed roles compel women to bear the "double burden": a relentless cycle of managing their household responsibilities while toiling for extended hours, all on meagre wages that can barely sustain their families. In both Assam and Tamil Nadu, for example, we found that men often resorted to consuming alcohol as a coping mechanism during the trying periods of state-sanctioned lockdown. Meanwhile, women were juggling caregiving duties and household chores alongside managing long work hours. Additionally, we also noted a substantial increase in the occurrence of gender-based violence. The intertwined socio-cultural, economic, political, and environmental aspects disrupted by the health crises and/or a disaster exacerbated the adversity faced by these vulnerable groups, where women bore the brunt of increased violence and over-exploitation.

Furthermore, despite being entrusted with household finances, women remained restricted in their independence in informal spaces. In fishing families in Tamil Nadu and Puducherry, women's assets, intended to provide them with a sense of autonomy, were routinely pawned to meet household needs, leaving them with little say in these decisions. The enduring issue of intra-household bargaining power persisted, with women having the knowledge of household finances but still remaining monetarily dependent on their husbands. This lack of agency hindered their ability to make decisions related to their own lives, health, education, and career opportunities, reinforcing the gender disparities deeply embedded in our society. The socio-cultural expectation for women to prioritise their family's needs over their own compounded the challenges they faced.

The lack of access to childcare facilities added further constraints to the lives of working women occupying informal spaces, inhibiting their ability to participate in the labour force. In Bhalswa, for instance, we found that while there may not be marked gender segregation, women continued to struggle due to a dearth of affordable childcare mechanisms. They were forced to segregate waste as well as fulfil their nurturing responsibilities. In fact, women, especially single mothers, were often left with no choice but to involve children in the segregation process, as it was difficult to separate them from their livelihood. Sadly, exposing children to the hazardous nature of waste picking has become a norm in Bhalwsa. This is because of the absence of institutional mechanisms that provide women with paid leaves or any job security. The limitations on women's working hours, aggregated with domestic duties, left them with little to no time for respite, underscoring the challenges of women's underrepresentation echoed in various informal sectors.

These disparities extend into the urban landscape, where women find themselves relegated to unorganised or informal sectors, highlighting the complex interplay of gender, mobility, and access. Women, constituting 88.8% of the industrial and 71% of the service sector of the informal labour force, confront substantial disparities in employment options

(International Labour Office, 2018). For instance, our ethnography in Kapashera revealed that the urbanisation process, resource constraints, and institutional biases perpetuate gender disparities. Women's lack of access to formal education and vocational training limits their opportunities, while societal norms enforce a gendered division of labour, further restricting their mobility. In addition to that, we found that there is an increasing demand for cheap labour, which attracts women to male-dominated sectors within these informal spaces; however, they remain at a distinct wage disadvantage. Women are often forced to work alongside their husbands but are seldom recognised as primary breadwinners.

The post-pandemic job market has been particularly challenging for women, who are often seen as liabilities due to their family responsibilities. The lack of job security made women reluctant to take time off, even in difficult circumstances. These exploitative working conditions were especially evident in industrial areas, such as Kapashera. Women were compelled to rely on precarious daily wage employment, resulting in a lack of stable livelihood and an absence of collective bargaining. These issues created insurmountable challenges for women, adversely affecting their health and well-being and hampering their autonomy. Despite facing challenging circumstances that are not conducive to work or exercising their agencies, women from informal spaces have tried to reclaim the narrative. Driven by the desire to be seen as equal to their male counterparts, women have striven to excel in traditionally male-dominated sectors, endeavouring to secure recognition for their labour. Reclaiming the narrative through collective support has become essential in the organisation of women in the workforce. This offers insights into the interplay of socio-cultural and political challenges and forces perpetuating gender disparities in informal spaces.

Therefore, to achieve gender equity, we require a comprehensive re-evaluation and unlearning of debilitating societal norms and structures to ensure that women are not only equal participants but also receive equitable opportunities and recognition for their invaluable work within these informal settings.

1.2 *Youth Choices and Trends*

In the wake of the post-80s neo-liberalisation era in India, a significant transformation in youth trends has unfolded, characterised by an increasing emphasis on consumerism and technology. The youth are at the forefront of this shift, harnessing the power of digitisation to navigate their aspirations. Adding to this, India's new middle class exhibits distinct aspirations compared to those from low-income backgrounds. For them, upward mobility often means securing a stable livelihood in the burgeoning service-providing industries, which are expanding rapidly within urban centres. This trajectory has led many young individuals to migrate to urban areas in pursuit of better opportunities and enhanced living standards.

However, a notable dissonance exists between the goals of the youth and the available job opportunities in both the government and private sectors. The government's ability to generate adequate jobs often falls short of the demand from the ever-expanding youth population, leaving many young individuals to explore entrepreneurial ventures and take calculated risks, even when their parents are engaged in jobs they could potentially inherit. We observed this trend in the fisherfolk of Tamil Nadu.

Our conversations with parents across studies also revealed that they realise the importance of education in a single distinct way. It is to improve the households' social and financial standing by enabling children to take up a distinct career path from their own or to improve the work that the household and the community at large engage in by disseminating the knowledge of their circumstances. The first case was more common across communities like the sanitation workers of Assam and the industrial colonies of Kapashera. However, the financial crisis, especially during COVID-19, caused a regression in the parents' efforts to achieve this as children dropped out of school and instead engaged in labour to sustain their lives.

This was noted in the case of the Bhalswa waste-pickers, wherein children segregated waste, especially in situations where parents were unable to work due to chronic diseases or prior injuries. Conversely, despite current adverse situations, parents intentionally steer their offspring away from their own professions, encouraging them to explore diverse career paths. This dynamic has led to an increased reliance on loans as a last resort to educate their children. If unsuccessful, this leads to a generational debt trap entrenching the household further into poverty. Young individuals who fall under the 18-year-old bracket, particularly those hailing from economically disadvantaged backgrounds, often do not possess the freedom to choose their preferred line of work, since it would be considered unlawful.

Youth forms the most populated demographic in India, thus making their choices a good forecast of the country's growth trajectory. With the advent of neo-liberalisation and the digital age, the trend of youth moving to the commercial and industrial sectors is more pronounced. What attracts the youth to these spaces are the formal conditions and the social status associated with these jobs as compared to their families' work. With this trend, sectors like fishing are witnessing a continuous decline along with an ageing population, jeopardising the loss of traditional knowledge and imbalance in the sustenance and sanitation workforce.

1.3 Income Choices

Despite the large, much-needed, spending on material goods for sustenance, it was observed that households spend a considerable amount on festivals and other alternate expenditures. Bourdieu's (1986) conception of the distinction between economic and social class can help in contextualising the choices made by these diverse, vulnerable communities. Even though they have limited economic capital, they desire to invest in cultural capital. This presents them with an opportunity to gain recognition and elevate their status in their community, as such investments are often identified as symbolic markers of success and prosperity. The habitus, influenced by their socialisation and societal expectations, guides their pursuit of cultural capital, reinforcing the complex interplay between social structures, individual dispositions, and the aspiration for upward social mobility.

In fact, we observed that in their quest to increase their social class, they even resorted to procuring loans from informal sources. Akin to Banerjee and Duflo's (2012) arguments in Poor Economics, we found that festivals and community gatherings held significant social and emotional value, compelling them to make "risky" monetary choices. This was especially evident in our interaction with small scale fishers of Tamil Nadu and Puducherry. They systematically invested in expanding their cultural capital by participating in community activities and supporting their children to pursue a career overseas. These choices reflect their commitment to preserving social bonds and securing informal support systems, which could later guarantee loans and other help in tough times (Portes, 1998).

In many low-income households, providing a good education for their children was a paramount objective. Education was viewed as a pathway to breaking the vicious cycle of poverty (Duflo, 2001). Despite limited financial resources, these marginalised families prioritised investing in their children's future. While this decision underscored their determination to improve the prospects of the next generation, we also observed that, across studies, this seemed to be the only investment the communities are in a position to make. Being forced to live on daily, often unpredictable wages, many of these workers faced the challenge of minimal savings, which left them vulnerable to financial shocks and unable to invest in opportunities for upward mobility.

Moreover, the prevalence of easily replaceable labour in these communities made workers risk-averse. This fear of unemployment limited their ability to demand fair wages (Kundu & Mohanan, 2009). This was witnessed in every case narrative apart from the self-employed sectors of fishing in Tamil Nadu. In addition to that, basic necessities like access to clean water consumed a substantial portion of their income, leaving little to no room for maintaining and replenishing savings (Gennetian & Shafir, 2015; Mani et al., 2013). Ultimately, the disparaging circumstances deprive communities of having a security net to fall back on when sudden shocks impact them. This highlights the constant financial juggling these households have to perform to meet their essential needs.

Overall, we noticed minimum savings among communities due to (a) not having official documents to access bank facilities and (b) continuously incurring health expenses and thus not being able to plan for long-term financial commitments. Defying common expectations, we found that the spending choices made by the poor involve social considerations beyond choices made for sustenance.

2 II

The trends and patterns we were able to map in this anthology were facilitated by the implementation of feminist ethnographic methods. As a part of practising the core ideals of feminist ethnography, we engaged in retrospective self-reflections. We pondered over the limitations of our approach and critically engaged with the endogenous issues that arose in the field determined by its informality. In conversation with the field ethnographers for the seven studies covered in this edited book, we inquired about the tenets of this methodology that guided them through the course of the studies. Ranging from gauging their motivations to the pursuit of activism, from interrogating accessibility to the question of men doing feminist ethnography, we have tried to connect with the ground realities of conducting fieldwork and negotiating different socio-cultural power hierarchies.

2.1 On Activism

In the realm of academic research, the pursuit of knowledge often walks hand in hand with the noble pursuit of activism. Feminist ethnography fundamentally seeks to unearth and challenge prevailing systems of power and oppression in social structures. It recognises the imperative need to shed light on the lived experiences of marginalised and oppressed communities, particularly women, and to subsequently foster a transformation. Moreover, feminist studies, by its very nature, is characterised by an unrelenting commitment to self-reflection and an acute awareness of the gaps existing in the researcher-researched dichotomy. During the pandemic, when theory was often met with pragmatism, the academic rigour of feminist ethnography could help in identifying isolated demographics during times of crisis, thus aiding activist pursuit.

Tavleen Kaur, a Research Assistant at the Centre for New Economics Studies (CNES), pointed out that in the pursuit of activism through research, there is a tendency to become captivated by grand narratives. However, an overreliance on idealism may hinder the research project's practical impact. To avoid such pitfalls, self-reflection becomes paramount. Kaur emphasises that the researchers must assess the feasibility of their ideas, keeping a fine balance between theoretical solutions and their potential to translate off-paper into plausible ground realities. The balance between idealism and pragmatism is one way to ensure that case study analysis produces tangible benefits for the community it seeks to give voice to. In addition to that, Kaur draws attention to the need for research projects to begin with a comprehensive understanding of the existing gaps between the researcher and the researched, as well as between research and policy(-making). By identifying where the disconnects lie, researchers can tailor their work to address these shortcomings. The ultimate aim is to ensure that research not only highlights the issues but actively contributes to resolving them as well.

In a related vein, Jignesh Mistry, a photojournalist at CNES, underscored the importance of community engagement. While activists offer valuable insights and narratives, it is equally vital for researchers to develop their own observations. While there is no denying that activist input is vital in grappling with the complexities, it is equally important for researchers to develop their independent perspectives by critically engaging with varied rhetorics that spread across the diverse stakeholders in the researched community's ecosystem. Effective engagement and collaboration with the community are crucial not only for the ethical conduct of research but also for ensuring that the community itself benefits from the research process. Despite this level of engagement, the lack of immediate and affirmative action poses an existential crisis for Siddharth G., the field ethnographer for the project on the fishing community. To soothe his anxieties, he approached the field with the motto of knowledge (re)production. Siddharth mentioned that while the outcomes of research may not always result in immediate, tangible change, they play an essential role in raising awareness—a form of activism.

The intersection of activism and academic research is a dynamic and multifaceted space. It requires careful navigation of various considerations, as exemplified by the insights provided by Kaur, Mistry, and Siddharth. While the pursuit of idealism is a driving force, the integration of pragmatism, self-reflection, and an awareness of gaps in research and policymaking are essential to ensure the research's practical impact. Engaging with communities and benefiting them in the process is equally crucial. Furthermore, the introspective moment Siddharth shared reminds us that research, even when it does not yield immediate change, can have a lasting impact on individual consciousness and societal awareness. It serves to underscore the point that research is an ongoing process, part of a broader dialogue, and not merely a means to an end. In essence, the confluence of activism and academic research is a challenging yet deeply rewarding endeavour. It necessitates not only methodological rigour but also a profound commitment to improving the lives of the communities under study. It is an ongoing dialogue that requires constant self-reflection, adaptation, and an unwavering dedication to making a difference in the world.

2.2 On Navigating Unpredictability and Making Research Accessible

A feature that is embedded within the feminist ethnographic approach is the essential task of navigating unpredictability while making research findings accessible to the community under study. Kaur perceptively highlights that the success of any project of this nature is contingent upon comprehensive preparatory work. The bedrock of such initiatives lies in diligent background research, which forms the intellectual scaffold for the subsequent inquiry. This preliminary stage is not one that can be hastily traversed, for it sets the stage for the entire research enterprise. Tavleen's advocacy for an in-depth understanding of the intricate interplay of diverse social forces and structures affecting the community under study is resoundingly germane. This understanding equips the researcher to be reflective and empathetic towards the lived experiences and social contexts of the subjects.

Laying the foundation for crafting questions enables the participants to take charge of their narratives, thus placing the power of storytelling firmly in their hands. The ethos of feminist ethnography is intrinsically linked to this principle, seeking to provide voice and agency to marginalised individuals. In this pursuit, it becomes imperative for researchers to disavow any hierarchical notions of their knowledge being superior to the experiential wisdom of the community members. The researcher's role is not to impose preconceived theories but to be a vessel through which the stories and experiences of the community can be shared and theorised. In essence, making informed choices in an unpredictable environment involves a deep engagement with the complexities of the community's social landscape, fostering reflective inquiry, and relinquishing the reins of narrative control to the participants.

Mistry's insights post-conclusion of a feminist ethnography project shed light on the imperative task of ensuring that the research findings are accessible to the community it seeks to benefit. This phase represents a crucial bridge between the academic realm and the practical world, embodying the essence of the research's impact. It is imperative to maintain open lines of communication with respondents so that they are not alienated from their efforts that facilitated the outcome of a research project. Transparency and openness in dialogue become the cornerstones of this process. When community members express interest in the research's outcomes and potential benefits, it becomes the researcher's responsibility to elucidate the intricate process behind the research.

Furthermore, Mistry alludes to the utilisation of digital tools, such as mapping, to make the research findings more discernible to the community. Once the team has processed and computed the findings from a research project, we work on articulating the results in a manner which is devoid of complex academic jargon and concepts. These are published in mainstream media and news houses, which make the results more accessible and relatable to the community. In fact, we often translate these articles into the community's regional language as well so that people from diverse faces of life have the opportunity to render the outcomes of the time and space they contributed for the benefit of the study. In addition to that, we also supplement these articles with visual aids, charts, and maps that can serve as informative resources for the community. The paramount goal is to demystify the research findings, making them accessible and comprehensible to those whose lives are intimately intertwined with the research subject matter. In this endeavour, the researcher becomes a conduit for sharing knowledge and reinforcing the collaborative nature of feminist ethnography.

While the pursuit of feminist ethnography underscores the importance of community collaboration, it is not devoid of challenges, as Mistry's inquiry alludes to. The harmonious collaboration between the researcher and the community members, especially when unexpected obstacles arise, can prove to be challenging. These may manifest in the form of resistance, reluctance, or scepticism from certain community members who may harbour apprehensions regarding the research's objectives or outcomes. Addressing such challenges necessitates patient, empathetic, and transparent communication. It is crucial for the researcher to not only be receptive to community concerns but also to adapt the research approach in ways that align with the community's needs and expectations. This may involve revisiting research objectives, methods, or ethical considerations to accommodate community feedback. Collaborative engagement is an ongoing dialogue that requires constant adjustment and a willingness to confront and navigate unforeseen challenges.

Feminist ethnography is an intricate and profoundly significant research methodology that strives to provide voice, agency, and social justice to marginalised communities. The central tenets of informed choices and accessibility, as elucidated through the insights of Kaur and Mistry, serve as guiding principles in navigating unpredictability while conducting research of this nature. Informed choices necessitate meticulous preparatory work and a deep understanding of the social forces at play within the community. It requires researchers to relinquish hierarchical notions and empower the community to take charge of their narratives. Accessibility, on the other hand, underscores the importance of transparent communication, open dialogue, and the utilisation of digital tools to unpack research findings for the community. Challenges may arise in collaborative engagement, but they call for patience, empathy, and flexibility in order to ensure that the research remains an inclusive and equitable undertaking. Ultimately, feminist ethnography stands as a profound and transformative research approach, bridging the gap between academia and the community, and championing the cause of social justice.

2.3 On Men Doing Feminist Ethnography

Feminist ethnography has long been regarded as a predominantly female domain, a research method rooted in the lived experiences and voices of women. However, the notion of whether men can effectively undertake feminist ethnographic projects is a matter of intriguing debate. Drawing from the perspectives offered by Kaur, Siddharth, and Mistry, this discourse delves into the multifaceted dimensions of this debate, emphasising the potential roles, challenges, and responsibilities associated with men engaging in feminist ethnography.

Kaur raises the pertinent point that feminist methodology, in itself, does not conform to a single, rigid definition of feminism. It encompasses diverse approaches, ranging from experiential perspectives to academic scholarship. The unifying thread, though, is the departure from objectivity and positivism. It underscores the necessity for a researcher to appreciate and internalise the need for subjectivity and the integration of lived experiences into research practices. A researcher who possesses a profound understanding of feminist methodology, irrespective of their gender, can embark on a feminist ethnography project. This underscores the inclusivity of the approach. It transcends the boundary of gender and invites individuals who align with the principles of feminist methodology to engage in the process.

On the other hand, Trisha, the field ethnographer for the study on the women of Kapashera, pondered over the challenges associated with men leading feminist ethnography projects. The primary challenge lies in the inherent biases that accompany a researcher's position in society. These biases stem from the societal roles and privileges attributed to individuals based on their gender. Men engaging in feminist ethnography may face difficulties in empathising with the struggles that may appear commonplace to women and non-binary individuals. The empathy gap can result in data that lacks nuance, as the researcher may not be attuned to the intricacies of the experiences being documented. Trisha aptly highlights that the very formulation of research questions can differ when posed by male and female researchers. The gender of the researcher can influence the depth and nuance of the interviews and the focus of the research, shaping the data accordingly. Therefore, the challenges of unbiased engagement are palpable when men undertake feminist ethnography, as they must confront and transcend the limitations imposed by their own societal positioning.

Siddharth's perspective adds a layer of nuance to the debate by emphasising the importance of recognising power dynamics and the need to (un)learn while conducting feminist ethnography. The act of research is a transformative journey, not only for the community under study but also for the researcher. Men can play an essential role in these projects by acknowledging and challenging their societal privileges and recognising the power they hold. By learning and unlearning, men can engage in the process of deconstructing the very power structures that may have previously benefited them. Siddharth's personal journey exemplifies the potential for men to become more nuanced and empathetic researchers capable of contributing to the field of feminist ethnography.

Mistry's insight underscores the interconnected nature of feminist ethnography with other academic disciplines. The feminist discourse does not exist in isolation; it intersects with various domains, including sociology, critical race theory, and critical legal studies. This intersectionality implies that men, engaging in scholarship related to these domains, can indeed make valuable contributions to feminist ethnography. It necessitates a holistic approach, acknowledging that feminist ethnography is not a separate realm but rather a complementary methodology that is informed by a spectrum of academic fields.

The question of whether men can effectively undertake feminist ethnography projects is a multifaceted one, encompassing issues of semantics, characteristics, and unbiased engagement. While feminist ethnography has traditionally been associated with women, the perspectives provided by Kaur, Trisha, Siddharth, and Mistry reveal that it is the principles of feminist methodology and the researcher's ability to engage empathetically and impartially that are paramount. Gender, though significant, should not be an exclusive determinant for deciding who can conduct a feminist ethnographic study. Feminist ethnography challenges us to re-think the heteronormative gender dichotomy by refuting gendered hegemony and power structures and helps in embracing the dynamism of the gender spectrum.

The delineation between insiders and outsiders in this conversation underscores the vital need for men to engage actively in researching gender issues, thereby challenging the notion that such inquiries should exclusively fall within the purview of women. This approach fundamentally serves to catalyse a transition from gender-blind to gender-sensitive methodologies, and, in doing so, unfurls the long and convoluted history of the "other" gender's marginalisation. The gender-sensitive approach, by design, acknowledges and confronts the pervasive societal expectations rooted in gender roles. Conversely, the gender-blind approach inadvertently negates the long, fraught history of the "other" gender in their pursuit of recognition and, therefore, impedes a nuanced approach to the equity discourse. Through feminist ethnography, men can find a platform for introspection and the recognition of their own positionality, enabling a heightened awareness of their privileges and an avenue for critical engagement with the broader gender discourse.

Thus, men can indeed contribute to feminist ethnography, provided they recognise their biases, commit to (un)learning, and approach the research with empathy and an understanding of feminist principles. In this way, the field of feminist ethnography remains dynamic, evolving, and, ultimately, a powerful tool for advancing gender justice and social transformation.

3 III

Our humble aim before embarking on our first project was to provide a platform for communities whose voices fell on deaf ears amidst the massive influx of (mis)information during the pandemic. As we expanded our team to include members with varying backgrounds and expertise, we became interested in the diversity in storytelling presented by different people in the research group. After analysing lived realities and rhetorics through audio-visual and photo-essay formats, our observations and findings have since been documented through media articles on the Wire, Scroll, and Quint, among others.

As Aimee Meredith Cox, in an interview with Davis and Craven (2016), articulated, "Is there a way to travel with the characters, to be more present in real-time with the interlocutors?", our inspiration was to present these narratives in a way that was led by informants and researchers in a symbiotic synergy. This endeavour sought to offer a novel perspective on ethnographers' experiences in the field, juxtaposed with their observations on and off-the-record engagements with respondents. This approach afforded us a fresh lens through which to view communities, transcending their conventional role as mere respondents to become integral components of the research process.

This anthology dove into these diverse informal communities in India during the COVID-19 pandemic. The stories we archived and analysed are of those who had to go out of their homes despite the lockdown and did not have the luxury of quarantining at home and enjoying an extended time away from work. In recognising and articulating that the pandemic's impact on these groups was based on a multitude of factors unique to their circumstance, we have tried to steer away from generalities and strive towards nuance and specificity.

We have, therefore, emphasised the profound importance of feminist ethnography in understanding the challenges and resilience of informal Indian communities. We underscore the need for researchers to balance idealism with practicality by reflexive thinking, prioritising accessibility, and transcending a singular narrative of destitution and helplessness, all in pursuit of a radical change in knowledge presentation and dissemination.

References

Banerjee, A., & Duflo, E. (2012). *Poor Economics: A Radical Rethinking of the Way to Fight Global Poverty* (Reprint edition). PublicAffairs.

Bourdieu, P. (1986). *The Forms of Capital* (J. G. Richardson, Ed.). Greenwood. https://home.iitk.ac.in/~amman/soc748/bourdieu_forms_of_capital.pdf

Davis, D.-A., & Craven, C. (2016). *Feminist Ethnography: Thinking Through Methodologies, Challenges, and Possibilities*. Rowman & Littlefield.

Duflo, E. (2001). Schooling and Labor Market Consequences of School Construction in Indonesia: Evidence from an Unusual Policy Experiment. *The American Economic Review, 91*(4), 795–813.

Friedan, B. (1963). *The Feminine Mystique*. Norton.

Gennetian, L. A., & Shafir, E. (2015). The Persistence of Poverty in the Context of Financial Instability: A Behavioral Perspective. *Journal of Policy Analysis and Management, 34*(4), 904–936. https://doi.org/10.1002/pam.21854

International Labour Office. (2018). *Women and Men in the Informal Economy: A Statistical Picture*. https://www.ilo.org/wcmsp5/groups/public/---dgreports/---dcomm/documents/publication/wcms_626831.pdf

Kundu, A., & Mohanan, P. C. (2009). *Employment and Inequality Outcomes in India*. Organisation for Economic Co-operation and Development. https://www.oecd.org/employment/emp/42546020.pdf

Mani, A., Mullainathan, S., Shafir, E., & Zhao, J. (2013). Poverty Impedes Cognitive Function. *Science, 341*(6149), 976–980. https://doi.org/10.1126/science.1238041

Portes, A. (1998). Social Capital: Its Origins and Applications in Modern Sociology. *Annual Review of Sociology, 24*(1), 1–24. https://doi.org/10.1146/annurev.soc.24.1.1

Index

D. Mohan et al. (eds.), *Pan-India Stories of Informal Workers During Covid-19 Pandemic*, https://doi.org/10.1007/978-981-97-1525-1

GPSR Compliance

The European Union's (EU) General Product Safety Regulation (GPSR) is a set of rules that requires consumer products to be safe and our obligations to ensure this.

If you have any concerns about our products, you can contact us on ProductSafety@springernature.com

In case Publisher is established outside the EU, the EU authorized representative is:

Springer Nature Customer Service Center GmbH
Europaplatz 3
69115 Heidelberg, Germany

The manufacturer's authorised representative in the EU is Springer Nature Customer Service Centre GmbH, Europaplatz 3, 69115 Heidelberg, Germany. If you have any concerns regarding our products, please contact ProductSafety@springernature.com

Printed and bound by CPI Group (UK) Ltd, Croydon, CR0 4YY
21/09/2026
02219995-0002